VARIETIES OF REFORM THOUGHT

3

H 4

V*arieties*
OF REFORM THOUGHT

Daniel Levine

MADISON

THE STATE HISTORICAL SOCIETY OF WISCONSIN

MCMLXIV

Library of Congress Catalog Card Number: 64–63188

Europe: W. S. Hall & Co., Inc., Amsterdam, London, New York
Canada: Harvest House, Ltd., Montreal
India: Thacker & Co., Ltd., Bombay

Publication of this volume was made possible by a grant from Lilly Endowment, Inc., Indianapolis, Indiana.

Printed in the United States of America by
WORZALLA PUBLISHING COMPANY,
STEVENS POINT, WISCONSIN

TO

Ray Allen Billington

Preface

While the historiography of the American Revolution, of Jacksonian Democracy, and of the Civil War has gone through many permutations, that of the Progressive movement is only in its second or third incarnation. Given time, historians will surely produce as many contradictory interpretations of this period as they have of other periods in American history.

Originally, historians of the Progressive movement saw reform between 1890 and 1914 as all of a piece. Populism, itself an outgrowth of Grange and Alliance, was the root of reform. From it sprang the trunk and limbs—the Square Deal espoused by Theodore Roosevelt and the New Freedom espoused by Woodrow Wilson. This view of reform is old enough to begin commanding new respect, but in general historians have discarded it. Scholars now treat Populism and Progressivism as distinct phenomena, with some overlapping of aims in the field of railroad and business regulation. Most of them regard Populism as rural-based and concerned only with gaining a greater portion of the national wealth for farmers. They view Progressivism as a more general attempt to adjust American institutions to a new urban, industrial age.

Interpretations of the ideology of Progressivism fall into three general groups. Some historians maintain that the reformers, having enjoyed an influential position in a society which they found to be essentially good, sought to preserve the old order, not to make it over. They reacted to those aspects of the new industrialism which distressed them by advocating conservative rather than revolutionary reforms. Tied as they were to the past, the Progressives were in a real sense reactionary. Among historians who see the reformers in this light, some approve of their attempts to preserve the old order, others do not.

An opposite interpretation holds that far from pining for a past age, the reformers were philosophers of a new ethic involving greater social unity and considerable governmental responsibility for the general welfare. Pointing to Progressive attempts to control business, protect the poor, provide social insurance, and extend social services, historians subscribing to this view contend that Progressivism was in fact the early stages of what later became the New Deal. The reformers appear to them as prophets looking toward the future, rather than as conservatives holding on to the past.

A third group of historians stands between the other two. These scholars refuse to admit that reform was all one thing or all the other. The reformers, they argue, can be divided into two groups, one tied to the past, the other to the future. Some historians indicate the difference by using the labels "New Nationalism" and "New Freedom," others talk about "Progressives" and "advanced Progressives," or "rural" and "urban" Progressives. Although aware of this divergence, these historians tend to regard the reformers as either predominately forward-looking or predominately backward-looking.[1]

Whatever the differences, all of these interpretations are syntheses. All seek patterns of beliefs and goals and categories of ideas around which Progressivism might be organized. The present work diverges sharply from this tradition by exploring differences and contradictions, variety and multifariousness within reform thought. I have adopted this approach because intellectual historians, perhaps more than some others, must constantly remind themselves that men's actions are not a very precise guide to their ideas. Federal regulation of corporations may appear to one man as a method of protecting a rural way of life, to another as encouraging small businessmen, to still another as promoting social justice for factory workers, to a fourth as asserting federal responsibility for national economic health, to a fifth as forestalling more radical measures.

Just as ideas are not precisely defined by actions, so ideas are not simply by-products of a particular environment. Lower-class city dwellers cannot be assumed to have the same ideas, nor do rural Midwestern lawyers share the same philosophy, nor do all men of great wealth. In short the intellectual historian distorts reality when he writes of an urban view, or a Southern rural philosophy, or a Midwestern outlook, or a working class viewpoint. The truth is that diversity, not uniformity is far more important in American life and thought than American historians have been willing to admit.

Diversity of philosophy, method, and objective merits particular emphasis during the upsurge of reform activity in the last decade of the nineteenth and first decade of the twentieth centuries. In this period reformers questioned traditional ideas and modes of action, and Americans generally looked more favorably upon social experimentation than in any previous period in the nation's history. Historians concerned with the Populist aspect of this reform activity are finding much diversity therein. The present work deals with diversity within non-Populist reform thought.

Intellectual historians have had a fundamental problem in defining the target of their research. Some have chosen to treat the ideas of a total culture as expressed in its customs and institutions. These scholars have narrowed the gap between intellectual history and social history. Other scholars have written histories of literature or philosophy. Granting that the history of philosophy is of tremendous importance, intellectual historians must also concern themselves with the ideas of men who were not primarily philosophers. Yet the intellectual historian need not therefore write social history. Intellectual history can concern itself with fundamental philosophic questions, but not confine its inquiry to philosophers.

Beside excluding from this study such professional philosophers as Herbert Croly and John Dewey, I have excluded reformers who might best be called dogmatists, people whose ideas can be described in a simple word or phrase, or who adopted a particular orthodoxy. Prohibitionists, vegetarians, and even socialists fall into this category. The individuals examined in this study worked out their own ideas. None of them accepted any previously developed orthodoxy.

To illustrate the wide range of fundamental social attitudes possible within the American non-Populist reform movement around the turn of the century, I have chosen five individuals and one organization. Each was at the center of some aspect of Progressive reform; none was attached to fringe groups within American society. Jane Addams not only participated in and publicized the movement for social justice, but she became a symbol for humanitarianism generally. Samuel Gompers gathered up the pieces of the labor movement after the Haymarket riot, then put them together in a new and viable form. The Civic Federation of Chicago became a model for men who wanted to bring virtue into civic affairs. Albert J. Beveridge, friend of Theodore Roosevelt, served as spokesman for what came to be called the New Nationalism. Robert M. La Follette, easily the best known and probably the most successful of the reforming governors, eventually emerged as the leader of Republican insurgency in the Senate.

Edgar Gardner Murphy is not as well-known as the other reformers. A quiet and modest man, his importance has been underestimated because he lacked the charismatic qualities and driving ambition of a Gompers or an Addams. Nevertheless, he helped bring non-Populist reform to the South, he endowed it with some of his own moral courage and personal warmth, and he gave reform the respectability it lacked in the hands of a Tom Watson. An ordained minister in the Protestant Episcopal Church of the United States, Murphy gave up his clerical collar in order to campaign against child labor, to improve Southern education, and to ameliorate relations between the races. Operating almost completely outside of the realm of politics, he spoke effectively for humanitarian reform in the New South.

As important figures in the burgeoning reform activity around the turn of the century, many of these leaders knew each other. All certainly knew of the others. Frequently various combinations of these reformers worked together for the same measures or the same candidates. With an exception here and there, they were allies in the same war. But they did not share a body of fundamental assumptions about man, society, government, and the good life. These people saw not the same social reality, but social realities of very different sorts. Jane Addams and Samuel Gompers might join in supporting the same strike, but they were in fact functioning in two different and in some ways incompatible worlds. Edgar Gardner Murphy and Albert J. Beveridge might join in opposing child labor, but their motives were quite different.

I have used the term "non-Populist" reformer to avoid what seems to me to be the fruitless question of whether these people were "true Progressives," "pseudo-Progressives" (as Daniel Aaron has called Theodore Roosevelt himself), or even "Progressives" at all. Each reformer treated in this study was consciously trying to adjust American life to the new industrial and urban environment. Each was regarded and regarded himself as a reformer. The word "Progressive" has been used in so many different ways that it has lost all clear meanings except as a designation for a particular time period or a particular political party. As a description of either an ideology or a political program I find it worthless and misleading.

Chronologically, this study begins in the early 1890's with the emergence of active and articulate non-Populist reformers. It closes somewhat more arbitrarily. By the end of William Howard Taft's term as President, and the election of 1912, Americans no longer argued about the need for reform, but rather about details of procedure. Reform had clearly triumphed both in politics and public opinion. This turning point provides a convenient place to end the study. Moreover, for some of the participants, 1912 marked an end of a phase of their own lives. Jane Addams and Albert Beveridge campaigned vigorously for Bull Moose candidates, but when the third party went down to defeat each turned to different activities. The Civic Federation of Chicago also abandoned general reform at about the same time. Edgar Gardner Murphy's health had restricted his activities after 1909, and he died in 1913. Samuel Gompers and Robert La Follette continued active in the changed climate after 1912; in their cases I have simply snipped the seamless web at that year.

The social reality perceived by each of these people can be reconstructed by analyzing the answers they gave to certain fundamental questions: What is the nature of man? Is he essentially good, in need of liberation, or essentially evil, in need of restraints? Are men rational? What motivates men? Are some men inherently more able than others?

What is the nature of society? Is it a single, unified entity, or are there sharp divisions within society? If there are divisions, are they based on race, class, nationality, or something else? Are the divisions good or bad? Can and should these divisions be altered? Should they be maximized or minimized? Are individuals being submerged by the groups of which they are members? Is this good or bad? Is city life or country life more productive of a healthy society? How can knowledge about society be gained? Should power in society be centralized or decentralized? Which is more important, liberty or equality? Can men change their position in society? Is government simply one of many institutions in society, or is it something transcendent?

How does society change and is social progress possible? How much? How fast? What is progress? Is change in society controlled by any one factor such as economics, divine will, or race? Should government be the agent for change?

What is the good life? Can it be identified with the farm

and small town, or is it a product of the metropolis? Does it involve strenuous competition, either within a nation or among nations? Is it based on greater co-operation and collective action? Is the good life contemplative, or active? Does the good life require material plenty, or does plenty sap the moral fiber?

Non-Populist reformers responded to these questions in various, complex, and contradictory ways. Any scholar attempting a synthesis of reform thought in this period must be aware of this variety and complexity.

This study began as a doctoral dissertation in the Department of History at Northwestern University. A predoctoral training fellowship from the Social Science Research Council enabled me to complete the dissertation, freed of other duties. I am grateful indeed for this support. Smaller grants from Earlham and Bowdoin colleges have also aided me materially. Portions of this book have appeared, in rather different form, in *Mid-America, The Indiana Magazine of History,* and the *Alabama Review,* whose editors I thank for permission to reprint.

Professors William Whiteside, Robert S. Maxwell, Claude Barfield, and Lawrence Parkus have read portions of this manuscript to my profit. Professor Robert Wiebe has gone over the whole manuscript with his unfailing critical eye. His comments have saved me from numerous pitfalls in methodology and content for which I am, although I may not have shown it at the time, eternally grateful. My debt to Ray Allen Billington goes far beyond the aid he gave me in preparing this particular book, and is indicated in the dedication. Needless to say, none of these people can be held responsible for errors of content or procedure that remain.

Daniel Levine

Brunswick, Maine
January, 1964

Contents

VARIETIES OF REFORM THOUGHT

Introduction

"What is man born for, but to be a Re-former?" asked Ralph Waldo Emerson, and Americans have never paused to reply, so busy have they been in pursuit of reform. Indeed, though American reform seems to swell and shrink in twenty-year cycles, Americans have rarely been without a substantial reform movement. The flood of political and social innovation of the Jacksonian era was continuous with the antislavery agitation which in turn became the Radical Republicanism of Reconstruction. The North was yet to abandon the Negro when the Liberal Republicans took up arms against Grantism. Liberal Republicanism of the 'seventies melted without division into the Civil Service reformers of the 'eighties and the good government movement of the 'nineties. The full flood of reform in the Progressive era left traces into the 1920's which were taken up and enlarged upon during the New Deal. If all men are not born to be reformers, America seems to have had her share of men who were.

This moil of reform has grown partly from Americans' confidence that things could and should get better, partly from a physical abundance which made tolerable the wastage of experimentation. Americans have been reformers partly because they have flattered themselves into thinking they had a special mission in the world and must serve as an example to those less blessed. Partly reform has been widespread because in the United States the cake of custom has been more easily broken than elsewhere. Elites have been less firmly established and more subject to infiltration. Partly it has been because the good life has appeared so close that any one ought to be able to share it.

3

In the Jacksonian era, reform was both political and humanitarian. Starting with the newer Western states, property requirements for the franchise were lowered or eliminated entirely. Jackson claimed he was bringing new groups to the upper heights of political power in the nation. Yet the lasting reforms of the "Age of Jackson" were as much social as political. Even the war on the Second Bank of the United States reflected, in part, a desire for the restoration of a simpler social order in which "monster banks" were unnecessary. In this quest for the "old republic" Brook Farm and New Harmony were only extreme examples, not an aberrant strain. For those to whom withdrawal to a planned utopia lacked appeal, the common school reforms of the 'thirties and 'forties offered a program of broad social betterment. The activities of Horace Mann in Massachusetts are the most famous of these efforts, but Mann was far from alone. In New York City, Philadelphia, and most of the states of the Ohio Valley, free elementary public education was made compulsory by law, though the laws were not always enforced. If the schools did not set all children on the paths of righteousness, perhaps the fate of those who strayed could be improved through prison reform. Some meliorists concentrated on ending imprisonment for certain offenses; others tried to improve the conditions of those already incarcerated.

If improvements in education and prisons would not bring on the millennium, allowing women their full rights as individuals and citizens might. Women should be permitted not only more sensible clothing, but also full rights in their own property and full participation in politics. The vote for women would bring them out of their narrow world of home and children, but more importantly it would infuse the political world with the virtues of the fairer sex. Perhaps even international politics might be cleansed of the moral offense of war. For, asked Charles Sumner in 1851, "Can there be in our age any peace that is not honorable, any war that is not dishonorable?"

Charles Sumner inveighed against war. Wendell Phillips

argued hotly for women's rights. Thaddeus Stevens' eloquent speech in favor of the Pennsylvania public education law saved the legislation from defeat. These are men more commonly associated with the greatest of all nineteenth century reforms, the crusade against slavery. Antislavery involved all the threads of the other humanitarian reform movements and added some new ones of its own. From the Lane Seminary rebels the crusade gathered evangelical fervor, from William Lloyd Garrison, a fierce passion for righteousness, from the Grimke sisters and the Quakers, a moderating gentleness. Extending from the futile gradualism of the American Colonization Society to the bloodthirsty fanaticism of John Brown, the antislavery movement aroused the nation as no other reform crusade had done.

Running beneath all these efforts toward change were the gentle voices of the Massachusetts transcendentalists. Emerson, Thoreau, and Alcott longed for a society closer to the natural order and less ridden by things. With the Jacksonians they wanted to recreate the "old republic" which had never been. Their romantic idealism provided still another viewpoint from which American society might be criticized. Yet their words helped to precipitate a war which brought about just the kind of society they most feared.

The humanitarianism of the antislavery crusade manifested itself in the Reconstruction period in the struggle to protect and enfranchise the freedmen. Yet the main thrust of reform in the quarter century after Appomattox focused neither on humanitarianism nor the extension of the franchise, but rather on economics and clean government.

The key to the economic changes after the Civil War was the railroad. Railroads in 1850 were relative newcomers to the carrying trade and had to compete against canals and established road freight companies. By the end of Reconstruction, tracks had been built beyond areas where canals or any other carrier could compete, and the railroad had triumphed as a hauler of freight. But where should this innovation be placed in American society? To what extent were railroads as common carriers subject to regulation by the public? What was permissible in the way of business organization, construction fees, rates, subsidies? Much of the reform effort in the decades after the Civil War addressed itself to these questions, first at the state then at the federal level.

Railroads were both a product of and a cause for the development of huge industrial corporations. They were the best customers for the burgeoning steel industry, provided the means to bring cattle from the Western plains to Chicago's packing houses, and carried the dressed meat all over the country. Wheat from the Great Plains and corn from the Ohio Valley could be shipped into Chicago for sale in the city's grain pit. The large corporations handling this commerce were the target of another of the post-Civil War reform movements. Economic and political institutions had to be readjusted to deal with corporate power. State regulation was tried and failed. Federal regulation was attempted only half-heartedly.

Huge corporations needing political favors threatened to corrupt American politics. As a result, a persistent theme of reform after Appomattox contended that honest government was the basis for all other improvements in American society. The performance of Grant's cronies, the fraudulence of railroad subsidies, and the notorious Tweed Ring all lent credence to the charges that government was shot through with favoritism, graft, and corruption. Much of the impetus toward Liberal Republicanism came from a growing revulsion against immorality in government and manifested itself particularly in the demand for reform of the civil service. Hayes attempted to bring honesty into the federal government, but made little headway before his term in the White House expired. Garfield's assassination by a disappointed office seeker gave the movement enough momentum to carry the Pendleton Act through Congress. Grover Cleveland, too, gave something more than lip-service to the ideals of a non-political civil service.

The 'seventies and 'eighties were the preparatory years for the reform movements which burgeoned in the closing decade of the nineteenth century. The Granger laws, the Interstate Commerce Act, and the Sherman Anti-Trust Act tried to curb the economic power of the great corporations; the Pendleton Act tried to eliminate the worst aspects of the spoils system in the Civil Service. After 1890 these reform movements coincided with a number of newer ones to create a great era of reform.

The struggle to regulate corporations found its most fervent expression in Populism. When high freight rates and a restrictive currency exacerbated the cyclical problems of crop failure and overproduction, farmers revolted, either inside their traditional parties or by forming new parties. The great depression of the 1890's injected new forms of humanitarianism into the reform objectives. This revived concern for human values took its place alongside the continuing demand for political and economic innovation. The New Urbanism, the New Industrialism, and the New Immigration combined to produce an oppressed group for whose protection traditional institutions had become inadequate. The combination of this new humanitarianism with the continuing efforts to regulate business and to cleanse government constituted the nucleus of the Progressive movement. In each of these three areas the Progressives went beyond their predecessors. The new humanitarianism continued the efforts of the Jacksonian meliorists to improve prisons and schools, but added a whole new set of attitudes and programs. The duties of society toward its most unfortunate members were redefined, partly by those attempting to uplift the downtrodden and partly by the downtrodden trying to lift themselves. Both groups insisted that welfare was not a matter for choice or a charity "which scrimped and iced, in the name of a cautious statistical Christ," but a matter of right. Both groups concluded that society must provide each human being with a minimum standard of living and that only the central government had the means to achieve this goal. Business regulation continued with perhaps less innovation during the Progressive years, though Theodore Roosevelt certainly sounded a note different to the one that Grover

Cleveland had sounded nearly a decade earlier. Moreover the aroused opponents of malefactors of great wealth, in arguing for more than they achieved, changed the climate of opinion in which business regulation took place. Advocates of clean government were no longer satisfied with programs of civil service reform, but insisted on bringing governmental policies under more direct control of the voters.

The coincidence of increased activity in the three areas of more direct democracy, more vigorous regulation of business, and an expanded quest for social justice created a flurry of reform activity unmatched since Jacksonian days. In some ways World War I was the climax of reform, and in some ways the first incident in a period of disillusion with the fundamental idea of social change. The 1920's did not entirely forget Progressivism, but other concerns took precedence.

Just as the depression of 1893 was the spark which ignited the Progressive fire, so the Great Depression of 1929 ignited the fires of a new era of reform. Old-time Progressives found their way back to Washington to work under Woodrow Wilson's former Under Secretary of the Navy, Franklin D. Roosevelt, some carrying old ideas with them, some with newer programs. There they met a younger group of reformers impatient with Progressivism and anxious to find new weapons to fight "old man depression." The experience of Progressivism plus the awesome severity of the depression meant that the New Dealers could go beyond the Progressives as the Progressives had earlier gone beyond their predecessors. An extensive system of private charity was not enough so social security legislation was enacted. Utilities regulation was succeeded by public power. Grudging acknowledgement of the rights of organized labor was followed by protective legislation for unions. The New Deal began with a program of fiscal orthodoxy, but ended by vigorously priming the economic pump.

In the decade after World War II, reform in America has been content to fill chinks in a house already firmly built. Extending social security, raising minimum wages, and erratically enforcing antitrust legislation provided no new direction for reform. Since 1954, reform has found a new "lead sector" in the relations between men of dark-brown skin with those of pinkish-grey hue. As yet, however, there are few signs that these efforts will inspire change in other areas of American life.

The Progressive years, then, those from about 1890 to about 1917, represent a culmination of old trends and the beginning of new ones. The ill-formed and halfhearted antitrust movement found vigor and direction. The forces of direct democracy flourished, then dropped out of sight. The welfare philosophy and the doctrine of the positive state found their first widespread acceptance. Some reformers worked within the church, some stayed away from churches. Some worked at the local and state level, some at the federal level. Some came from the upper classes, some from the lower. Some tried to preserve an old society, some to hasten a new world. Some started with economic concerns and hoped to change the quality of American life. Some started with politics and hoped to change economics. For varying periods of time large numbers of people coming from different directions and having different destinations found themselves on the same road. Looking about them and seeing a multitude, they concluded they were part of an army. This bit of self-deception gave them confidence in their strength, but we should not allow it to deceive us.

1

REFORM AND SOCIAL UNITY

Jane Addams

The various roads toward reform began as footpaths well before the era called Progressive. One of the most important of these roads started as an inchoate Christian humanitarianism, and had its direction determined by the great changes taking place in American life in the last decades of the nineteenth century. The economics of these changes is easiest to measure: an increasingly rapid industrialization, ever larger corporations formed by growth or merger, increased gross national product. Demographic changes were necessary concomitants: greater proportion of people in cities, which were rapidly increasing in size. The other side of the coin of demographic change is social change. As cities increased in size, a new form of society was created in the United States, one made up of vast numbers of industrial workers living in close proximity to one another and to their places of work. In addition, vast numbers of immigrants poured into the city. By the last decade of the century an increasing proportion of them were so-called new immigrants. No longer were the newcomers relatively skilled, relatively well-to-do, and relatively assimilable natives of Britain, Germany, and other parts of northern and western Europe. Now the immigrants were the impoverished natives of Italy, Russia, Greece, and other countries of southern and eastern Europe. They further complicated an already complex social system in the poorest districts of urban America.

America's cities were not equipped to deal with this prob-

10

lem. There was not even any widespread acceptance of the idea that the cities had the responsibility of dealing with it. The resulting chaos was not all bad. For many, immigrant enclaves within the great cities served as effective way-stations between European and American life. Years later first and second generation immigrants often looked back nostagically to the lower east side or "Little Italy," where they had once lived. Indeed, the slums often formed benign self-policing communities.

Yet the slums produced more than nostalgia and honest homespun philosophers. Filth, disease, overcrowding, inadequate diet, and other products of poverty brought great human misery. Americans, confronted with these inescapable phenomena, slowly revised their thinking about the nature and causes of poverty.

Throughout much of the nineteenth century, Americans had assumed that poverty, while perhaps not a necessary part of civilization, was a natural outgrowth of the varying abilities of different men, and therefore, very little could be done about it. Toward the end of the century, a new attitude became evident, which saw poverty not as the result of individual differences, but rather as a by-product of an evil economic system or an evil social system.[1]

At the same time, the definition of poverty underwent an important change. Until sometime toward the last quarter of the nineteenth century, poverty was defined as simply having nothing, as being on the verge of death through starvation or exposure. Toward the end of the century, charity workers and others investigating the conditions of the poor, became convinced that not only the dying needed help, but also those on the edge of impoverishment. More and more these observers concluded that being poor was not an ennobling experience, but a debilitating one. The proper recipients of charity were not only the totally helpless, but also "those having too little of the common necessity to maintain themselves at their best."

If poverty, a debilitating condition of life, was the result of environment, clearly something could and should be done about it. Ready at hand was the new science of society, which might be able to do something. Along with new ideas about the causes of poverty there grew up a more systematic approach to its cure. Data were gathered by people who made careful studies of working men and their families. A growing professionalism and secularism replaced the haphazard religious administration of relief. New workers flooded the field of charity work: professors making surveys, case workers employed by civic agencies, factory inspectors, administrators of child labor laws, and founders of settlement houses.

Like many social reforms in the United States, the settlement house movement began in England. The movement was closely related to the newer attitude toward the causes and definition of poverty and to the newer ways of dealing with it. Settlement workers were concerned not only with the completely dependent, but also with those in a state of debilitating yet not desperate poverty. These workers usually began as amateurs, with no very clear program in mind, but they soon developed a professional competence in a wide variety of fields. They worked closely with the academic disciplines of sociology and economics and contributed to both disciplines. Jane Addams' ideas were in tune with these newer attitudes and her work was instrumental in giving them force and making them effective.

Like virtually all founders of early settlement houses, Jane Addams spent her early years far from the squalor of the slums. She was born and grew up in the tiny town of Cedarville, in northern Illinois. Her earliest recollections involved her father and Cedarville, for both the person and the place exercised an important influence throughout her whole life. John Addams, Jane's father, had brought his young bride to the banks of the Cedar River in 1844, where he planned to follow his trade of miller. His move from eastern Pennsylvania to northern Illinois brought him from the old settlements around Philadelphia to near-pioneer conditions. Sparsely settled, the land around Cedarville held great possibilities for the future, but its present was uncertain. Its greatest economic need was transportation. Abundance could come from its gently rolling hills but the market was in Chicago. Proposals were made for dredging streams and building canals but John Addams put his faith in railroads. Traveling up and down the country, he helped organize the Chicago and Galena Union Railroad. This not only got the railroad built, it also made John Addams a well-known figure in northern Illinois. Ten years after his arrival he was elected to the state senate, an office he held first as a Whig, then as a Republican until he voluntarily relinquished it in 1870.

John Addams was probably the most prominent citizen of Cedarville and his daughters might be forgiven if they regarded him with some awe. For Jane, the youngest of the four children who lived beyond babyhood, John Addams' character was more important than his achievements. He was a Quaker, a faith he chose by conviction rather than upbringing. His Quakerism implied a sternness which seemed cold to those who were not close to him. A man of firm conscience, John Addams knew his road by following an "inner light." Although Jane Addams was never formally a Quaker, she shared with her father a sense of an "inner light" which she knew led her toward righteousness. It was from John Addams that she absorbed a strong sense of duty and a concern with the moral values expressed by her society. She revered her father and gave him her "doglike devotion." She wished her hands, like his, would become speckled from sparks flying from the millstones. She often woke at three o'clock in the morning, as he had as an apprentice. She started to read through the scanty village library, as he had done, and she felt herself unworthy to be his daughter.

Jane hardly knew her mother, who died in 1862 when Jane was only two. For five years Jane's eldest sister ran the household and the entire family deferred to the wishes of baby "Jennie." Suddenly, or so it must have seemed to a seven-year-old child, a new mother appeared with two sons of her own. John Addams had remarried. Jane and her step-mother maintained a formal cordiality but the two never really got on. Soon the eldest stepbrother returned from his medical studies in Germany and married Jane's older sister Alice. Both parents opposed the marriage, which only took place after a series of long and bitter family arguments. Such bitterness was created that the young couple moved hundreds of miles away and never again lived near their parents.

At the age of seventeen, Jane followed her sisters to Rockford Female Seminary. Her performance at Rockford was outstanding. She had nearly perfect grades, was editor of the college magazine, and even studied taxidermy on the side. She graduated first in a class of seventeen young ladies. At Rockford, the vague sense of duty toward society which she had inherited from her father, was given more definite direction. The Seminary in the 1870's was a veritable breeding ground of missionary young ladies. The school hoped to send its eager evangelists to all corners of the heathen world. A good deal of pressure was put on Jane Addams to become a missionary to Turkey. She not only resisted this pressure, but she even refused to become a communicant of one of the Christian denominations. However, she did take seriously both Christianity and the missionary ideal that a Christian had responsibilities in this world. By the time of her graduation she had determined to help people in body rather than soul. She would become a doctor.

In the summer after her graduation, John Addams took his daughter to Wisconsin, where he was investigating a possible investment in land. Without warning he was stricken with acute appendicitis and within a few hours he died. A cheerful journey with her father had turned for Jane Addams into the supreme tragedy of her life.

For a few months she continued with her career plans. In the fall of 1881, she entered the Women's Medical College of Philadelphia. There a slight congenital spinal curvature began to bother her, and under the academic strain, the shock of her father's death, and her increasing discomfort, she collapsed. After spending a few weeks in a Philadelphia hospital, she returned home for six months of convalescence. She never attempted to return to medicine.

After this physical breakdown, her brother-in-law, by then a surgeon, operated successfully on her back. He also prescribed a trip to Europe, normally a standard occurrence for young Misses Addams. This was the first of two trips which Jane Addams took during the course of the next half-dozen years. Although this first trip was largely occupied with an avid search for Old World culture, it also helped direct her toward the kind of reforms which were to absorb her whole life. Along with the beauty of the Old World, she saw in somehow starker relief than she had at home, the difference between affluence and poverty. It was the poor of London's East End who, at least in retrospect, stayed most in her mind. She attended an auction of nearly spoiled food on a Saturday night where the starving poor could buy a decaying cabbage for a farthing or two. Most of all, she was impressed by the outstretched hands reaching, almost in supplication, for what the rest of society was discarding as unfit. These sights affected her profoundly, but did not furnish her with a guide by which she could direct her life. She had a strong and conscious desire to do something, but she did not know in what direction to turn. Although she became a Presbyterian in 1885, she would have nothing to do with missionary work. Her enthusiasm for medicine had died after seven months and she still lacked a purpose.

She returned to the United States in 1885 and spent two years drifting in and out of Baltimore society. Too serious to be content with the social whirl, yet too undecided to do anything else, she was deeply discouraged. Finally, in the winter of 1887 she returned to Europe in the hope of finding what she had missed on her first trip. At Munich she joined her close friend from Rockford, Ellen Gates Starr. On this second European trip she found her direction. The compassion she felt and the need for greater unity of the human family suddenly seemed to suggest only one path to her. She must go and live among the poor—be a neighbor to them. At first she was hesitant to speak of her idea, but slowly she disclosed it to Ellen Starr, who encouraged and finally agreed to join her. After a quick trip to London to look at Toynbee Hall and Walter Besant's People's Palace, she returned to the United States to make her home among the poor of Chicago.

What determined the direction of the road which led Jane Addams to Hull House and social reform? Her personal and family life certainly was an important factor. Worshipping her father, she never found a man to equal him, or her image of him, and as a result never married. Without a family of her own, she devoted herself to a broader human family in the neighborhood around Hull House. In addition, John Addams' stern sense of duty and righteousness was transmitted in undiminished strength to his daughter. Heightened by the atmosphere at Rockford, which was pervaded with the desire to cleanse and purify the world, this sense of duty might well be turned toward some form of beneficence. Jane Addams perceived, earlier than most people, that the most pressing need for beneficence was in the burgeoning cities. Not content with traditional charity, Jane Addams learned of the settlement idea in England and determined to try it in the United States. Once in residence at Hull House in Chicago, the problems of her neighbors brought her into one reform movement after another, at an ever-accelerating pace.

She was a reformer of great effectiveness. The number of subjects upon which she concentrated and in which she gained a professional competence was enormous. She was at home discussing housing statistics, the economics of child labor, the best methods of education, proper diet, and many more. In all of these areas her actions were efficient and effective in producing the results she wanted. In her own terms she was a success, for she increased the unity of American society.

All of Miss Addams' actions, from her first tentative experimentation at Hull House to her later work for international peace, were directed toward the ideal of human unity. This ideal, that between man and man no barriers could exist which their common humanity did not overwhelm, was for a half century the guiding force behind her life.

Her conviction of the unity of humanity was based on a view of man as essentially good, and life as essentially beautiful and joyous. Children had a natural sense of this joy and beauty which adults, except artists, lost. Adults, to fulfill themselves, must regain this sense "which does not consist in wealth, in learning, in enterprise, in energy, in success, not even in that modern fetich [sic], culture but in an inner equilibrium, in 'the agreement of the soul'."[2]

This untainted goodness of youth expressed itself in a natural desire to help the unfortunate, and a divine drive toward the constructive and healthy. Instead of exploiting this drive, however, adult society suspiciously regarded it as naïve altruism. If given the opportunity, Jane Addams felt sure that children would prefer healthy athletics to smoking, drinking, and gambling. Between the ages of seventeen and twenty-three, this divine drive expressed itself in youth's burning desire to perfect the world. Modern society should cherish these impulses and take every opportunity to employ them.[3]

Miss Addams also saw other levels of human motivation. There were deep unconscious drives in human beings which could explain their actions. One of these was the need for food, "the hunt developing into war with neighboring tribes, and finally broadening into barter and modern commerce; the second urged him to secure a mate . . ., widening into the building of homes and cities, into the cultivation of the arts and a care for beauty."[4]

The very early years of life were of crucial importance. Once set wrong as children, the road to joy and beauty was difficult to rediscover in adulthood. In speaking of women who had become prostitutes at least partly because of parental neglect, Miss Addams wrote "one knows that, whatever may be done for them later, because of this early neglect they will always remain impervious to the gentler aspects of life, as

if vice had seared their tender minds with a red-hot iron."
Throughout life, too, the environment must encourage rather
than frustrate natural instincts. A working girl who had
stolen money for a wild spree was sent to prison "to expiate
not only her own sins, but the sins of those who had failed
to rescue her from a life of grinding monotony which her
spirit could not brook."[5]

Hull House always concentrated its efforts on the children
of the neighborhood. At times this might take the form of
lobbying for laws against night hours for newsboys, or
against child labor of all sorts. On a more regular basis it
meant supplying children with an atmosphere which would
open their minds to the gentler aspects of life: competitive
sports for the boys to take the place of running wild in the
streets; cooking and sewing clubs for the girls; drama and
singing for boys and girls.

The environment which most frustrated human instincts
was the city. Men in cities, Miss Addams thought, were like
cats in a mouseless office. Just as the cat would play at hunt-
ing mice with bits of paper and string, so men in a nature-
less city needed recreation which would simulate the process of subduing nature, and thus give them the illusion, if
nothing more, of being masters of their fate. Perhaps re-
calling with nostalgia her early years in rural Illinois, she was
sure that a rural life was man's natural calling. Country
work was far more normal than life in a factory. The personal ties of a small town were more natural, where even
courtship took place under the protective community eye.
Anyone who had such a pastoral simplicity in his early life
had a haven of memories to which he could retreat from the
horrors of a city. She wrote of a "drunken man, in a maudlin
stage, babbling of his good country mother and imagining he
was driving the cows home and I knew that his little son,
who laughed aloud at him, would be drunk earlier in life
and would have no such pastoral interlude in his ravings."
The city divided men from each other and thus made them
too weak to cope with their environment.[6]

Miss Addams tried to cope with this lack of communication in two ways. She gave children a taste of a more whole-

some rural life at the Hull House Camp known as the Bowen Country Club. There children could substitute a surrounding of shady trees and bubbling brooks for one of back alleys and garbage cans. Her other method was to make Hull House a communication center both for the neighborhood and for the city as a whole. This meant forming clubs where men of common interests or backgrounds might meet. Perhaps more significantly it meant providing neutral ground where men of conflicting interests might meet. Strikers and their employers often worked through a Hull House intermediary, sometimes Jane Addams, sometimes another resident. One nationality group might make its first contact with other nationalities at Hull House. City officials often came to Miss Addams to find out conditions and opinions on the West Side, and if they did not come to her, she went to them.[7]

Nor was the city alone in destroying the goodness and joy in modern men. The United States was in a period of "intense and over-wrought industrialism" which had taken all joy out of work and life. The blot of the factory system was such that whole neighborhoods could be denied any experience of youth's joy simply because the young people went into factories. The industrial system also swallowed up the charms of recent immigrants. Jane Addams, perhaps with regret, realized that the days of a rural America were gone forever. She asked for an awareness of the human cost of industrialism and for some more equitable division of that cost.[8]

This industrial system had produced false values. With the tenacity of the well off, Jane Addams would not admit that success in life meant material abundance. People must be measured in human terms such as kindness and generosity. Youth especially must not be subject to "commercial standards" and used up in hard labor.

Poverty was one result of the modern industrial system. Each person played such a small role in the economy that the economic machine could function without him. Therefore, many people were helpless and could be driven to poverty through no fault of their own.[9]

Crime too was a result of the unnatural city environment.

Most crimes could be forgiven because "the humble people sin through weakness and passion but seldom through hardness of heart." These sinners should be treated with the mercy of the founder of Christianity. Along with Judge Ben Lindsey and Clarence Darrow, Jane Addams favored a policy of rehabilitation rather than punishment.[10]

The city environment could even distort the basic drive toward securing a mate. This drive could lead to a deep devotion between individuals and indirectly to an appreciation for beauty. The city, which quickened the sexual impulses of youths without providing an outlet for their energy, drove them into vice of all varieties.[11]

The most dangerous result of an urban industrial environment was what Miss Addams called group morality or class consciousness. In sharp contrast to some other reformers, she regarded all such impulses as destructive. Loyalty to class was nearly as bad as loyalty to self or to one's family. As opposed to group morality, she argued for a "larger conception of citizenship" embodying the good of all groups.[12]

In sum, the fault of modern society was an alienation of man from man. Her solution was to assert by word and deed the unity of humanity. A society which denied this unity denied the natural order. Her task, she felt, was to bring society back to that natural order.

Human beings were bound together, she felt, primarily by their own psychological needs, for "no one can safely live without companionship and affection. . . . It is as if we had to build little islands of affection in the vast sea of impersonal forces lest we be overwhelmed by them."[13]

In some ways this unity was a heavy load to carry, for each person became responsible for the sins of all. "This is the penalty of democracy, — that we are bound to move forward or retrograde together." On the other hand, the feeling of unity with all of humanity could be an enriching experience, as certain elements in the trade union movement were beginning to find out.[14]

This concept of social unity, of a society in which there were no barriers of class, occupation, or social standing between individuals was Jane Addams' ideal. Yet she herself was from that very class which she felt was, through well-being, losing its contact with the common run of humanity. During the first years at Hull House, she made a conscious effort to cast out the devil of social distinctions in her own mind, yet she never quite reached her ideal. In writing to one of her closest friends, Mary Rozet Smith, she referred to Miss Smith as a lady but to the recipients of charity as girls, then catching herself, she added, "excuse the false social distinction, a remnant of former prejudices."[15] In spite of her best efforts, however, remnants of former prejudices were not completely exorcised.

One aspect of these prejudices was a Thoreauan view of the poor as possessed of a peculiar charm and wisdom denied the well off. Wisdom, Jane Addams thought, often resided in the hearts of the simple, who had "charms and resources undreamed of by the upper classes." Indeed, living as they did on the very edge of disaster, the poor "have constant opportunities for self-sacrifice and generosity. . . . This is their reward for living in the midst of poverty." These opportunities taught the poor, earlier than other classes, the necessity for economic co-operation rather than competition. Therefore, the beginning of the new "humanitarianism" to take the place of the present "industrialism" was manifested among the poor. Eventually, a day was coming when the affairs of men would be regulated by these "simple people, who carry in their hearts the desire for mere goodness, who regularly deplete their scanty livelihood in response to primitive pity, and . . . who have an unquenchable desire [for simple justice]."[16]

Jane Addams' class consciousness was not wholly a matter of respect for the noble poor. She also retained former prejudices of the type which regarded the poor as in some ways worse than other members of society. She never stopped being a "lady" no matter how ashamed she may have been of using such a term, and dinner was generally a rather formal occasion which, while perhaps omitting fingerbowls, omitted very little else.[17]

Probably unknown even to herself, Jane Addams looked condescendingly on her neighbors. Charity, she insisted, should not consist of forcing the poor to emulate the rich, yet her choice of words in making this point betrayed her. She said that it was as wrong to expect a poor man to act like a rich one as it would be to expect a child to act like an adult. Besides, one could hardly expect the "same human development of an Italian peasant and a New England scholar." In the first instance and in much the same way that one expects that a child will eventually become an adult, Miss Addams' choice of simile evidenced an attitude which expects a poor man eventually to behave like a man of means. Moreover, her choice of polar opposites in the second instance assumed that New England scholars were superior to Italian peasants.[18]

Nor were differences between rich and poor purely a matter of background and environment. Perhaps differences in education could account for the fact that the rich could respond to intellectual appeals like books and lectures, whereas the poor needed drama and personality to be affected. Sometimes, however, Miss Addams doubted whether the poor could ever be brought out of their poverty, lacking as they did that "social energy which makes for progress." In a discouraged mood, she wrote to Henry Demarest Lloyd that she respected his faith in what working class people could do, and added, "living with them does not always give one this view." She even believed that "the inherent uncleanliness of their minds prevents many men from rising above the rank of day laborers."[19]

Jane Addams' attitude toward foreigners was similar to her attitude toward the poor. On the one hand she praised Old World values. Indeed, one function of Hull House was to keep alive the traditions of the old country and to help convince the second generation to "have a respect for the older cultivation, and not quite so much assurance that the new was best." Thus the "Labor Museum" at Hull House preserved the techniques and tools of Old World civilization: a distaff from Greece, hand looms from Bohemia. Miss Addams felt it was wrong to Americanize immigrants to the point where loyalty to the old country was swept aside. Italians with the tradition of Mazzini, Garibaldi, and Cavour could cherish both their older tradition and the newer patriotism of Washington and Lincoln. Moreover, Americans should recognize that immigrants often had a different value system, one that it might be worth preserving. Under this system, a Russian talmudic scholar should be respected even if he could not speak English or get a decent job. In some ways, Old World customs might even be better than American ones. For instance, Miss Addams was not at all sure that the village settlements of Italy were inferior to the American system of farming isolated quarter sections of land. She opposed any restriction on immigration, arguing that American ideals were broad enough to include all who wanted to come, and that the United States should continue to act as the haven for all the world.[20]

On the other hand, Jane Addams sometimes betrayed an attitude of condescension toward recent immigrants. She had no doubt that Americans were inherently superior to the newcomers. The "primitive habits" of newcomers should not be allowed to interfere with American traditions. Immigrants must be willing to learn from their hosts who "represented a distinctly superior standard of life and thought." America was engaged in building a new civilization and immigrants should be proud to take part in the task and not to cling too closely to their European ideas.[21]

There was a third aspect of Jane Addams' thought which implied a contradiction with human unity. This was her belief in moral evolution. Individuals and societies, she thought, evolved morally just as species evolved physically. If men evolved morally, it was possible that not all men were at the same stage of moral evolution at the same time. Some people were morally superior to others. At one end of the scale were primitive people like south Italian peasants. At the other end was the "intellect" of, perhaps, a New England scholar. Here again was a belief in precisely that kind of social cleavage which Jane Addams so vigorously denied.[22]

In spite of these remnants of former prejudices, Jane

Addams directed her whole life toward achieving her ideal of human unity. She firmly believed that progress toward such achievement was possible. Sometimes she saw evidence that the world was not moving in the right direction at all. Writing in 1909, she saw a moral decline, a world sunk in a materialistic morass, without moral standards. She felt that her society was losing its human concern in a quest for "commercial ideals." In spite of periods of doubt and discouragement she continued to work toward her ideal, and deep within her was a firm core of belief in "the modern evolutionary conception of the slowly advancing race." Believing in evolutionary moral progress did not lead her to accept the inevitability of progress by any process akin to natural selection. With Lester F. Ward she believed that men could and indeed must direct their own moral evolution. "The world grows better," she said, "because people wish that it should and take the right steps to make it better."[23]

Thus, while much of Miss Addams' writing was concerned with the faults of her society and while hers was an effective voice for viewing with alarm, her aim was always positive. She pointed out faults not for condemnation, but correction, and she had a very clear idea of how this correction should be achieved. Her approach to the correction of flaws in the social fabric was strongly influenced by the new science of sociology. In the first textbook on sociology, Jane Addams' close associate, Albion W. Small, wrote that "sociology was born of the modern ardor to improve society." At the same time, the ardor for improvement was given a powerful increment by sociology. Miss Addams' approach to social ills was to "readjust the social machinery" in such a way that conflict would be eliminated in favor of a higher type of social unity. She assumed that there was a social machinery and that it could be manipulated to achieve a desired result. This does not mean that she was willing to forego human sympathy in favor of a cold scientism, but simply that normal impulses of compassion must be systematized to become more effective.[24]

The first step in this process was the accumulation of

data. These data were far from impartial. They were always chosen to illustrate a point, and the conclusions were in hand before the investigation was begun. Often a dramatic anecdote might be more important than a carefully compiled list of statistics. Nonetheless, the techniques developed in the service of reform could grow into a new science. From Hull House and other charitable institutions flowed a steady stream of detailed information about Chicago. *Hull House Maps and Papers* was a large compendium of detail on wages, ethnic groups, occupations, and the like in the area around Hull House. Through such efforts, Miss Addams was sure that the reasons for crime and vice could be revealed, then cured.[25]

Proceeding on the basis of carefully compiled data, much could be done by charity. Since charity was to be based on sociology, it could best be administered by professionally trained workers, whose training supplemented but did not submerge normal human emotions. Charity workers had as one of their purposes the task of caring for "the wounded in the unequal battle of modern industry." They were also "to make the entire social organism democratic," which to her meant the elimination of social and economic barriers. Crossing as they did class and social borders, charity workers had a duty to interpret various groups to each other. If this could be done, then perhaps the Americans could be kept from going berserk over an "anarchist" bombing. In other words, charity workers in a pluralistic community had to be the conscience of the nation, keeping each group from the throat of its neighbor and all from mass hysteria, a function Miss Addams herself frequently performed.[26]

But charity was basically a manifestation of human sympathy and therefore could benefit the charity worker as well as the recipient. The charity worker could satisfy her natural urges toward helping others and would, like the master in Tolstoy's "Master and Man" who perished that his servant might live, be "filled with an ineffable sense of healing and well-being." The danger in this was that the charity worker might concentrate on her own satisfaction, on "being good" in her own eyes and those of her neighbors, more than she concentrated on social amelioration.[27] At times Jane Addams herself may have fallen prey to this danger.

In this charitable work, Miss Addams gave women a special place. In dealing with the place of women, she frequently mixed her social views with self-justification. Having rejected, or been unable to partake of family life, she was reluctant to regard the family as sufficient for emotional fulfillment. Women, she felt, shared with men a responsibility beyond their family to "the State and to society in the larger sense." In fact, she could not find adequate justification for family life within the family itself. The sacredness and beauty of family life came from "sharing the corporate life of the community and making the family the unit of that life. Thus women, especially college women who have been exposed to a wider view of life, could not allow themselves to remain only in the home. To do so was to ignore the "social claim" or the "race claim" on each individual.[28]

Charity then, with women playing a leading role, was one way in which progress toward her ideal of human unity might be achieved. Charity, however, was only preventive or corrective. Reform, Miss Addams thought, must also directly foster the good life, must "increase the positive value of life." The great evils resulting from industrialism and the city could only be dealt with, she felt, through education. "Until the educators take hold of the situation the rest of the community is powerless." Much of Jane Addams' thinking on the goals and methods of education parallels in a somewhat less sophisticated form, that of John Dewey. Schools, she insisted, should not simply teach the basic tools of literacy, but should "free the powers of each man and connect him with the rest of life." In a nation being flooded by immigrants from a wide variety of backgrounds, where thousands of rural families were flocking to the cities, in a nation not yet accustomed to industrialism, she argued for a greater emphasis on what have since come to be called social skills.[29]

How were these goals of education to be reached? Miss Addams, from her experience with children at Hull House, thought that the starting point for all education must be with the child's own experience. The school should teach him the place of this experience in his society and should show him how to direct his experience to fit better with the experience of others. From this starting point in the past, education should go on to the future, teaching children about the life they were going to lead. For most children, this life would not be that of a professor, or even of a clerk, but rather that of a factory worker. Therefore, education should concentrate on what would best fit children from working-class neighborhoods for a working-class life. Although this could be accomplished in part by technical training, more was needed. The drudgery of factory life came not so much from repeated operations, but from the fact that each man's job seemed to be only remotely connected with the finished product. Education for workmen should teach the contribution of their operation toward the finished product and the place of these products in the total economy. Partly Miss Addams' views were simply a realistic acceptance of the facts which faced children growing up in an industrial district of Chicago. One might well argue that a Polish immigrant working in a meat-packing plant had no need to learn Latin. Yet the conclusions she reached would have had the effect of educating workers to be workers and keeping them in their place. This could have led to extremely rigid class lines and just that sort of "group morality" against which she protested.

Women, too, should be educated in a special way. Women, like workers, were not going to be scholars. Therefore, their education should not concentrate on "intellectual accumulation," but rather on the cultivation of those "larger desires of which all generous young hearts are full." In a word, women should be trained as settlement house workers.[30]

The most important institution for fostering the good life, however, was neither charity nor education but government. Jane Addams admired, besides her father and

Abraham Lincoln, a romanticized image of Mazzini. Like Mazzini, she saw the State as possessing some sort of a transcendent existence. The State was a mystical entity above and beyond the institutions and individuals which composed it. The State grew out of, or was, that mass of general principles upon which its citizens agreed. It was thus that entity which bound all its members to itself and to each other. Yet growing out of the ideas of its citizens, the State was also society manifest. It embodied the collective will and the collective conscience.[31]

If the State was society manifest, then it was imperative that the various organs of government respond to the collective will. Jane Addams felt that a great danger for the twentieth century would be to lose faith in the ability of the people to run their own affairs. She was sometimes convinced that the Founding Fathers themselves lacked this faith. Expressing an idea later made more explicit by Charles A. Beard, she believed that the Constitution had been drawn up on the basis of English law to protect property rights. This was done in a nation for which these English laws were irrelevant, and in thus drawing the fundamental law, the Fathers had failed to provide adequate methods for the expression of the popular rather than the proprietary will. Along a somewhat contradictory line of reasoning, she argued that the American political system had been devised on purely political grounds with economic affairs being ignored. Since then, however, the common life had ceased to be political and and had become economic. As society manifest, the State must respond to these changed conditions and "not remain motionless, enchained to a degree of civilization attained [by a previous age]." Therefore, government had to deal with economic conditions brought about by the new industrialism. She was even willing to live with political corruption, although she deplored it, if the corrupt politician dealt with the daily economic problems of the people. Through the State, then, the conscience of society could be brought to bear on social and economic problems. Without government, philanthropy was ineffectual; with government, anything could be accomplished.[32]

Jane Addams saw an even greater role for government than that of society's conscience or a supreme agent for reform. She argued for a welfare state more inclusive than anything that was to appear for over half a century. Government should not simply concern itself with the wicked by punishing them and the destitute by helping them. These extreme cases were happily in a minority. Government should also take an interest in the great mass of the population in its normal everyday occupations. "We care with tenderness for the defective and the dependent," she said, "but for that great mass of people just beyond the line, from whom they are constantly recruited, we do practically nothing." Here she was setting forth a new definition of the needy as not only those on the verge of death but all those who could not adequately fulfill their own destinies. If most of the people were to fall short of full success in the struggle of life, then the government surely had an obligation to deal with these near-failures. That government in the United States was far from accepting these responsibilities was shown by the extent to which private groups had to exercise welfare functions which were in fact societal responsibilities.[33]

Societal responsibilities began with food and housing. Miss Addams felt that it would not only be humane, but actually economical for government to set minimum standards of nourishment and housing and to support people at this level, rather than to allow them to sink into abject poverty. Beyond this minimum, each municipality had responsibilities for the emotional and moral well-being of its members. Conditions of labor and disputes between labor and management should also be determined by the government. In short, there were few aspects of life toward which Jane Addams did not feel government had a prime responsibility.[34] In return, each individual had responsibilities to the State, that is, to society. These duties forbade every individual, every family, and every group from concentrating on its own well-being.

Miss Addams worked toward her objectives through all levels of government. In times of unemployment in Chicago, she urged the city to supplement private relief. Hull House had a nursery to care for young children of working mothers, and Miss Addams was delighted when the city took over part of this function. At the state level she lobbied in Springfield for all manner of laws, some to prevent abuse, others to provide more education and welfare. Her political activity culminated in her support for Theodore Roosevelt's Progressive party in 1912. Carefully ignoring Roosevelt's militarism, and the elements of opportunism in his bolt from Republicanism, she seconded his nomination at the Chicago convention, and campaigned across the nation for his election. She saw in the Progressive party the realization of all her ideals: a national party which preached federal responsibility for the general welfare. She was convinced that if the Bull Moose program, including Woman Suffrage, was enacted, morality would triumph in American life.

It is clear, therefore, that Jane Addams was above all a moralist, but a moralist on her own terms. Her fundamental appeal was not to practicality, to tradition, or to godliness, but to a humanistic ethic. On occasion she referred to her ethics as Christian, but she carefully emphasized that she meant no present Christian church, but "the original primitive communal (and completely tolerant, self-sacrificing and self-effacing) kind" of Christianity. Ethics for her, concerned not man's relation to God, but to his fellows. Religion must connect itself to the daily lives of its communicants, and for her any faith which turned its fervor to social ends was fulfilling its purpose. The cosmos beyond man held very little interest for her. She felt that ethics were undergoing a revolution and that she must help bring this change to pass. Thus ethics was for her, not an unchanging body of precept to be approached more or less closely by succeeding generations. Rather ethics consisted of the necessities demanded by the circumstances in which each generation found itself. Here again, we arrive at the basic root of Jane Addams' social philosophy—the concept of human unity. She felt that in the twentieth century individual righteousness was not enough. Being moral in this new era meant having what she called a "social ethic," a sense of responsibility toward society. Morality consisted in having this sense and acting upon it, immorality meant a concentration on either self-aggrandizement or individual salvation.[35]

In sum then, Jane Addams believed that somewhere deep within every human soul, obscured by urban industrialism, lurked a kind and benevolent nature thirsting for fundamental communication with the rest of humanity.[36] The good life could be reached by nourishing this thirst for communality, by clearing away all barriers between men and stamping out the individualistic ethic which had raised these barriers. There were three methods by which this goal of social unity might be furthered. The first was charity, which could alleviate immediate suffering and provide a nucleus of people whose allegiance was to society as a whole rather than any part. The second was education, which could show workers reasons for satisfaction in even the most humble task and teach women how to exploit their natural, humanitarian impulses. The third, and by far the most important, was government. As the conscience of society, as society manifest, government had a prime obligation to each individual not only to provide certain political rights, but also the basic economic and social necessities for satisfactory living. In return, each individual must contribute toward the advancing welfare of the whole social organism.

Thus, although Jane Addams was neither socialist, anarchist, nor communist, she was a radical. In fact, she was more radical than any of these three groups. Not only did she demand an all-pervasive welfare state, she also demanded a drastic change in human actions and morals. Not sharing the Marxian conviction that a change in institutions would bring a changed morality, she wanted both changes to come at once. As the State adopted more welfare functions, the individualistic ethic should be discarded and the social ethic adopted in its place.

In some ways this was a long way from Cedarville, Illinois, and Rockford Female Seminary. However, few people really outgrow the ideals of their childhood. The ideals of her father and of Rockford, when placed in a Chicago slum, could quite easily emerge as a belief in the welfare state. Indeed, by 1912 the growth of reform along lines of which Miss Addams approved, indicated that many Americans shared at least parts of her ideals. Yet her goal of human unity was not the only possible response to the distress of the urban poor. Many reformers who fought side by side with Jane Addams in some of her most important battles were not animated by her desire for a classless society.

2

REFORM AND SOCIAL CONFLICT

Samuel Gompers

Samuel Gompers had no memories of harmonious village life to contrast with his urban experience, for he never lived outside the city. Jane Addams' years in Cedarville provided her with a model for a better, more benevolent society whose virtues she hoped to bring to an urban setting. She saw the seeds of this kind of society in the labor unions, where co-operative effort could promote general welfare. Almost invariably she took the side of the workers against their employers. Jane Addams accepted conflict between social classes as a temporary—if perhaps necessary—evil. Samuel Gompers, by contrast, not only accepted social conflict as necessary and inevitable, he thought it far from evil. Indeed, he believed that social progress could frequently spring only from social unrest and disharmony. Gompers and Jane Addams supported the same strikes, such as the famous Hart, Schaffner and Marx strike in 1910, and they shared common short-term goals. Fundamentally, however, they lived in different worlds and disagreed about ultimate objectives.

They came from different worlds too. The crowded, sooty, industrial sections of London and New York were his Cedarville. The Spitalfields area of London's East End was not a poverty-stricken slum, but it was poor. There, three generations of Gompers lived in the three-story house where Sam grew up.[1] His grandfather, who had brought the family from Holland before Sam was born, lived on the top floor and conducted a trading business between England and his homeland. Samuel's father had inherited neither the taste nor the ability for business. Instead he became a cigar maker, and never developed entrepreneurial ambitions. Although the family was Jewish, it did not observe the ritual of its religion strictly. Nevertheless, it kept the high holidays and Samuel received his only schooling, four years of elementary education, in a Jewish school.

During the early years of the American Civil War, the cigar-making trade in London fell upon hard times. Cigar makers, along with workingmen throughout the city, saw more and more of their fellows forced into the growing ranks of the unemployed. In 1863, partly in the hope of finding steady work, Samuel, then fourteen years old, emigrated with his family to America. In New York, Samuel and his father first worked at home making cigars for a jobber, but soon the son found a job in a factory. In 1864 he joined the English-speaking cigar-makers union, and from then until his death sixty years later, he proudly maintained his membership.

Gompers gained much of his education in cigar factories. A quiet and fairly routine operation, cigar making lent itself to talk. In many shops, instead of aimless talk, one of the men would read to the others who would give him a few cigars each so he would not lose pay. This custom prevailed especially in shops filled with German cigar makers, many of whom were refugees from post-1848 reaction. As with many poor but earnest seekers after truth, Gompers turned to the Cooper Union for history, biography, music, and various more practical subjects, but he received the core of his education in cigar factories. Here, among widely read men, Gompers came into contact with the broad stream of European liberalism. Here his eyes were opened to the dimensions of social problems and social protest. Here he toyed with and rejected socialism, and here he formed his convictions on the self-sufficiency of the trade-union movement.

In all his activities, Gompers seems to have been a natural leader. A quality of confident assertiveness made him speak up whenever something troubled him and his fellows generally respected his opinions. They elected him president of various fraternal organizations, and wherever he worked they chose him as their unofficial spokesman. His confidence and assertiveness grew with him. In his old age, after years of having had his views accepted as being right, he became unable to admit any other possibility. His confidence eventually became pure cussedness.

His natural qualities of leadership gave him an increasing influence among cigar makers, a trade long used to unionism. In 1875, Gompers became president of Local 144 of the Cigar-Makers International Union of America. Initially attracted to the radical unionism of the First International, by the 1870's he had abandoned revolutionary ideas for the less grandiose objectives of the Cigar-Makers. With this union he learned the strategic lessons which were to guide him as president of the American Federation of Labor: how to strike; when to negotiate; how to talk with and influence politicians. He became convinced that economic pressure, not politics, was the most effective means for improving the conditions under which men worked.

The years from 1875 and 1886, which Gompers spent learning the techniques of trade union leadership, were extremely difficult ones for the American labor movement. Dissatisfied with any of the European patterns of organization, American workingmen could find no program which was both strong enough to be effective, yet consonant with their rejection of European radicalism. For a time the answer seemed to have been found in the Noble Order of the Knights of Labor. Begun among Philadelphia garment workers, the Knights had grown only slowly until the great railway strike of 1877. The bitterness of this strike created a temporary feeling of solidarity among American workers which the Knights were able to transform into increased membership. Under the leadership of Terence Powderly the Order evolved a patchwork method of organization and a broad set of goals. Reflecting a preference for the industrial over the craft form of union organization, and paying little attention to the development of a coherent basis for association, the Knights accepted as member unions workers of one nationality, of one shop, of one area, of one trade, or of several related trades. The aims of this conglomerate federation included not only higher wages, shorter hours, and better working conditions, but whatever political and social goals member unions espoused. Eventually this loose, irrational structure caused their downfall. Member unions often had temporary fits of enthusiasm which left behind nothing more than shrinking membership lists. The Knights reached their peak in the mid-'eighties, then went into decline.

To the left of the Knights was a squabbling group of socialist organizations. Each claimed to espouse the true faith, and most seemed more intent on destroying rival socialists than on bringing about the downfall of capitalism. Chief among them was the International Workingmen's Association founded by Karl Marx in London. To the right of the Knights of Labor was a small, weak group with a long name: the Federation of Organized Trades and Labor Unions of the United States and Canada, which emphasized craft unionism, a modest political program, and economic goals.

The victory by the Knights in a controversy with the Wabash railway in 1884 seemed to establish them in unassailable command of the American labor movement, but two years later, the Haymarket riot in Chicago sent a wave of anti-labor sentiment across the country. Starting as a peaceful meeting in support of strikers at the McCormick Harvester Works, the Haymarket affair became a bloody riot when a bomb exploded in a group of policemen. Within a few minutes ten people were killed and fifty wounded. In the popular mind the tragedy identified labor organizations with violence, and in the bitter reaction which followed trade-union influence and power declined sharply.

At the same time a series of quarrels with the Knights made craft-union leaders receptive to the idea of a new organization. In December of 1886, representatives of craft unions met in Columbus, Ohio, with officials of the Federation of Organized Trades and Labor Unions and formed the American Federation of Labor. In searching for an executive officer, the new organization looked for a man committed to craft unionism, experienced in leadership, opposed to labor in politics, and above all, willing to administer an organization lacking both funds and, apparently, prospects for success. Largely because he possessed the latter qualifications, Samuel Gompers was elected president, a post he was to hold, with the exception of one year, until his death forty years later.

Although the Knights of Labor declined after 1887, the AF of L grew only slowly. Until the 1890's its survival was problematic and the depression of 1893 provided a critical test. By managing to cling to at least a skeletal organization until prosperity returned, the AF of L survived the crisis. It soon won a few spectacular victories and by the turn of the century had assumed unquestioned leadership of the labor movement.

More than any other factor, the AF of L owed its success to Samuel Gompers. At the base of his leadership and tactics lay a social philosophy which contrasted sharply with that of Jane Addams. Gompers had an all encompassing class consciousness. Particularly before 1900, his class consciousness was even more pervasive than that of Karl Marx himself. When Marx turned his ideas into action, he gladly accepted aid from any quarter. Gompers, however, suspected and scorned all but genuine wage earners. He believed that only two classes existed: "we" and "they," the "worker" and the "capitalist," between whom yawned an unbridgeable chasm. Class consciousness, an inevitable and useful product of the gulf separating the classes, meant that "those who belong to the class are conscious of the fact and are conscious, too, of the fact that their interests as a class are separate and distinct from any other class." Class consciousness of this type especially disturbed Miss Addams.[2]

Gompers saw class warfare as an inevitable outgrowth of class consciousness. Because the workers had only their labor to sell and almost completely lacked power, they could never have any real harmony of interests with their employers who purchased labor in the same way that they purchased any other commodity and who wielded great economic and political power. The triumph of employers in the late nineteenth century, Gompers thought, had created a tyranny more oppressive than that of medieval noblemen. "By stealth and subtle scheming, the wealth possessors of our country have endeavored and are endeavoring to retake from the masses the rights that have been dearly bought, secured and guaranteed." Against this rapacious class of wealth-absorbing capitalists, workers had to wage constant war.[3]

Gompers thought of himself less as a reformer than as a military commander in this incessant class war. He used military terminology constantly: invade, march, column, skirmish, enemies. He viewed labor as a nation within a nation threatened on all sides by enemies. Using a Darwinian metaphor more commonly associated with businessmen, he argued that labor could achieve "success in the struggle for existence," only by remaining armed and alert. To defend themselves, workers had to band together. They had to recognize the "imperative necessity of the twofold unity of trade and class." Every manifestation of "a growing spirit of solidarity" within the working class gave him pleasure.[4]

For Gompers, a major purpose of trade unionism was to promote this spirit of unity. Unions, he wrote, "led men toward the upper heights of working class unity." Even an unsuccessful strike could be useful if the very act of striking strengthened loyalty, self-sacrifice, and fellowship. Fired by a new feeling of solidarity, workers would help their fellows in time of need. They would not only go on strike and contribute to strike funds, but would also help other workers in time of sickness, accident, and unemployment. With Jane Addams, he asked that each person be guaranteed a minimum standard of living. However, where Jane Addams wanted society as a whole to guarantee this minimum, Gompers wanted the working class to guarantee a minimum to its own members.[5]

Like Miss Addams, Gompers rejected the doctrine of the rugged individual making his way in a hostile world by the force of his own abilities. He too insisted that "we cannot live alone, we are social beings." He too maintained that "the excellence of the individual is not the secret of progress. Civilization is but another name for cooperation, mutualism, common effort. Individuals in isolation, however excellent they may be, are impotent." Nevertheless, where Jane Addams believed that co-operation between social beings would eliminate social and economic barriers, Gompers merely envisioned using co-operation to strengthen class solidarity. No effective, homogeneous group, he contended, could be larger than an economic class, and he bluntly informed Henry Demarest Lloyd that no person could really understand the point of view of a class to which he did not belong.[6]

The necessity for class solidarity meant that each worker would have to give up a little of his own freedom for the good of his class. Gompers knew that closed shops, organizational picketing, and boycotts limited individual freedom. But each worker owed to his class the acceptance of these limitations.[7]

Gompers' class consciousness led him to conclude that every institution, including government, was either a friend or an enemy of labor. The government of the United States, Gompers was convinced, was an enemy. "Under the present form of government," he said, "more rights have been filched from the people than [under] any other form." Government by the people and for the people was a sham, for the government was simply an appendage of the enemy capitalist class.[8]

If government served the opposition, workers could best serve their interests by keeping government out of economic affairs. In this respect, Gompers assumed a position perhaps more laissez-faire than that of big business. He called his opponents "pseudo-individualists." Throughout the 1890's he hammered away at the theme that the eight-hour day could best be won through economic pressure on employers, not through law. The abuses of trusts could be cured by labor solidarity, not government. Arbitration might be useful, but compulsory arbitration was simply a disguised method for depriving labor of its economic power. Even unemployment should not be dealt with by government; the labor movement should care for its own.[9]

Unions had to remain apolitical if they were to keep government out of union affairs. In any case, union involvement in political activity diverted energy from the class struggle. Moreover, Gompers had seen several labor parties fail and in failure destroy the unions which had overreached themselves. In the 1890's his opposition to union participation in political activity was complete. Unions should simply stay out of the "miasmatic atmosphere of political party corruption." He counseled "masterful inactivity" in the election of 1892, and he excoriated both the Knights of Labor and the socialists for trying to involve the labor movement in politics.[10]

After 1900 Gompers continued to urge labor to "hold fast to that which has proved to be good," such as staying out of politics, but his opposition to political involvement began to waver. He did not abandon his devotion to class warfare, he simply decided that government, as a weapon of opposition, had to be blunted. Despite this gradual shift in strategy, he never believed that government could rise above the class battle to serve society as a whole. Nor did he abandon his belief that labor's salvation lay in successfully waging class war. As early as the 1890's Gompers had encouraged individual workmen to support candidates and measures which might help labor, but he regarded such activity as merely peripheral skirmishes between the classes. The AF of L took more concerted action beginning in 1906 by presenting its "Bill of Grievances" to Congress. Although this tentative step into politics seems to have had no tangible results, political activity increased during and after the panic of 1907. A lengthy monthly "Report of the Legislative Committee" became a regular feature in the *American Federationist.*[11]

Gompers abandoned the doctrine of non-involvement in politics not because of economic conditions, but because of a decision of the United States Supreme Court. The Danbury Hatters' case in 1908 made unions liable for damages caused by a boycott. The decision threatened the very basis of unionism as Gompers believed it should be practiced. If the decision were allowed to stand—or worse, extended to prohibit all collective economic activity—it would destroy the labor movement's only effective weapon. Gompers, outraged by the decision, attacked its soundness in law and logic in the longest editorial of his career. He concluded with a plea for congressional relief. A month later his plea had changed to a threat and within three months he went so far as to ask, "What power should the workers use if not their political power?"[12] In the twenty years preceding the Hatters' decision, Gompers had consistently expressed the contrary view—that the workers had nothing to gain by involving themselves and the labor movement in politics.

Though Gompers now took a less jaundiced view of political activity, he justified political action only so far as it aided his cause in the class war. Gompers asked Congress to strike down the court decision in order to allow labor to use its economic weapons. However, like a fly in a spider web, the more he struggled to be free, the more deeply he became enmeshed in politics.

Despite Gompers' distress over the Hatters' decision, it was not yet certain that aroused labor would become partisan labor. Gompers approached both major parties in 1908 asking their views on the Hatters' case, on amending the Sherman Act to exempt unions, and on other matters of direct interest to labor. Finding the Republican party cool but the Democratic party seemingly receptive, he soon urged union members to "respond in hearty sympathy with the Democratic party." From 1908 on, Gompers' annual reports to the AF of L convention contained increasing amounts of explicitly political material. By 1912, while still insisting that there had been no change in policy, he filled the pages of the *American Federationist* with political editorials. He endorsed the Democratic party, repudiated the Republicans, and very nearly ignored the Progressive party. By 1912 Gompers had followed the route of most men who want social change in the United States; he had found himself unable to avoid working through the federal government.[13]

While Gompers frequently derided the government of the United States, he felt a genuine loyalty toward his adopted country. He shared the common American notions of disentanglement from Europe and of America's superiority and mission. "There can be no doubt," he wrote, "that to the workers of America falls the mission of leading the great movement for amelioration and emancipation." "The old world is not our world. Its social problems, its economic philosophies, its current political questions are not linked up with America. . . . In the procession [toward social justice] America is first."[14]

Inevitably, Gompers' class consciousness tempered his patriotism. Like the Marxists he regarded imperialism and war as red herrings introduced by a few selfish men to distract the nation from internal economic problems. Territorial expansion was simply a capitalistic search for cheap labor. Wars enriched the capitalists while the workers, who were naturally allies rather than enemies, bore the cost. Ostensibly, he subordinated his patriotism to an awareness of the international solidarity of the labor movement, but in reality he refused to sacrifice immediate gains in the United States for an international goal.[15] When war actually came to the United States, Gompers' class consciousness, opposition to war, and sense of solidarity with the working classes of all nations did not stand. Like the leaders of working-class movements in most countries, he could not resist pressures toward nationalism and patriotism and he vigorously supported America's war effort.

Samuel Gompers' racism was as much a part of his class consciousness as were his attitudes toward government and war. While making statements supporting equality, he always placed union strength ahead of racial equality. This was well illustrated by an incident involving two AF of L organizers in New Orleans, John M. Callahan, white, and George L. Norton, Negro. Callahan was something less than co-operative with Norton, who himself was resented by the white workers he attempted to organize. Gompers wrote to both men pleading for harmony between them. To Callahan he said that Negroes must be organized or they would underbid organized workers. To Norton he insisted that while he never made distinctions between black and white, effective organization was more important than racial parity. He advised Norton to avoid contact with men who would resent him, and to concentrate on organizing Negroes. Gompers was even more vicious when he spoke of Orientals than when he spoke of Negroes. He insisted that the Chinese were inferior and unassimilable. His ultimate appeal, however, was the economic argument that Chinese workers would undercut American workingmen.[16]

From the earliest days of the AF of L up to and beyond World War I, Gompers held consistently to the view that although discrimination based on race or nationality was wrong, non-discrimination must give way to trade-union organization. He warned Negroes against being cheap men, and insisted that "the Caucasians are not going to let their standard of living be destroyed by Negroes, Japs or any other."[17] Coming from an immigrant Jew such sentiments might seem strange indeed, but Gompers, sharing the racial assumptions of most Americans at the turn of the century, and faced with the federated organization of the AF of L, had neither the power nor inclination to insist that the labor movement eschew discrimination. Besides, the essence of his philosophy of social action was that one thing should be done at a time. To others he left the task of achieving racial equality. He set himself the task of winning the class war.

Gompers was convinced that the war was being won. Progress, he maintained, was the natural law of society. There was no such thing as the "good old times." The present was the best that had yet been, and the future would be better. But progress toward a just and better world did not occur without vigorous human effort. The effort began with discontent which Gompers said was "the greatest factor in progress." Society was given a powerful nudge along the path of progress when the discontented elements rose up against oppression. "Liberty has never been conceded to people," he said, "liberty comes from power, and conscious power, and that conscious power intelligently and humanely wielded."[18]

Not a revolutionary, Gompers wanted no apocalypse to bring on the millenium. "All progress, to be safe, is necessarily or apparently slow." He was even suspicious of too rapid growth in union membership, feeling that if growth were headlong it might not be permanent. He favored a gradual improvement, one step at a time, and he opposed the Marxian belief that things had to get worse before they could get better. It was true that in the face of vigorous opposition gains could in fact be made only in small steps, but Gompers accepted gradual progress not because no alternative was available to him, but because of a deep belief in a naturally functioning, progressive universe whose advance was a product of class strife.[19]

Thus progress became for Gompers a matter of how best to use the limited power at his command. Power should be applied to its fullest extent. In answering a query as to whether a union might fine a non-member for scabbing, he answered, "It is a matter of power, where the union has the power it can and should punish the crime of scabbing." However, unions must be careful not to extend their efforts beyond their effective power. Frequently he cautioned locals, especially newly formed ones where enthusiasm outran resources, not to rush into a strike, and to accept less than complete victories. "Justification does not always lead to successful strikes. You must not only be right, but must possess the might and be able to support your right."[20]

Knowing the limits of his power made Gompers all the more aware of the need for strategic application of his slender resources. His theory was to maintain a pure, hard core of troops who could most effectively hit hard at narrow objectives. A strong class consciousness was the first requirement for his troops. In part the union itself could contribute to this spirit if the union were made

> protective in its character. In other words . . . members of the Union should be required to pay higher dues into the Union, and to receive a considerable benefit from it thus to inlist [sic] the material interests of the members in the Union; not so much for the sake of the material interest, but for the sake of keeping them in the Union. When that is once secured, progress can be made in any direction.[21]

Gompers simply did not believe that the trade-union movement could afford to worry about those who were either unwilling or unable to pay high dues. A closely knit, loyal group was for him far more important than a large amorphous association.[22] Coming from a craft union, these ideas seemed natural, but eventually proved inapplicable to the mass industries where workers demanded the protection of unionism on a scale far larger than anything the AF of L was prepared to provide.

The purity of his hard core was essential to Gompers. While he acknowledged that "the best and most marvelous achievements in the world took shape first in the brain of some dreamer," he opposed the membership of intellectuals and theorists in the AF of L on the grounds that their ideas might be "splendid . . . even glorious, but they are not war—that is, the war of labor for labor's rights." "The emancipation of the workingmen must be achieved by the workingmen themselves."[23] To be sure, Gompers had other reasons for denouncing intellectuals. On one level he felt that he must explicitly disengage himself from radicalism. By denying ideology and theories, he said in effect that he was neither a socialist nor an anarchist. On another level, he had to convince his followers that he was still a workingman, even though his function appeared managerial. To this end he maintained membership in the Cigar-Makers long after he had ceased to make all but a few ceremonial cigars. By rejecting the help of professors and theorists, he was declaring that he was not of the leisured classes. Like oil and water, workers and intellectuals could never mix.

On similar grounds, Gompers regarded charity as a divisive force which lured workers away from militant unionism. He was glad of the public support charity workers might give the trade-union movement, and in times of extreme emergency he demanded a dole to keep men from starving, but charity was only a partial and inadequate substitute for higher wages. Workers did not need this "grudging and meager dole" but wanted to achieve justice through their own efforts.[24]

Gompers' strategy of throwing hard-core troops against a limited objective enabled him to build out of the shambles of Haymarket a labor movement which survived depression, the Pullman strike, and war.

Samuel Gompers, then, was not one of those Americans who started with the assumption that man was essentially good, in need only of liberation from this or that constriction to create a heaven on earth. His basic assumption about humanity was that people were, and ought to be, selfish. Every person and every class wanted to increase its grasp of the world at the expense of others. For the working class starting from a deprived position, such grasping was simply a quest for justice. Resistance would come from those who already had more than their fair share, and the ensuing struggle would result in social progress. Power, and he seemed always to mean economic power, was for Gompers the ultimate motive force in society. A shrewd manipulator of power, he slowly, and with no major error, built a viable labor movement.

And yet, radical though his terminology may have been, his goals were mild and familiar. He wanted greater material welfare for workers, greater freedom for them to determine their own destiny, and thereby greater self-respect. Ever wary of being tarred with the brush of radicalism, he refused to speculate about Utopia.[25] The economic system, the social system, might stay as they were. When Gompers said he wanted "more, more, more, now!" he may have sounded rude, but he did not sound radical, for what he clearly meant was "more of the same."

Thus Samuel Gompers' approach to the new urban age was an attempt not to moderate conflict in pursuit of a co-operative image, but rather to exploit conflict for the benefit of his class. For him, industry and the cities which industry created offered a new arena for an age-old struggle.

3

REFORM AND THE STATUS QUO

The Civic Federation of Chicago

The battles, the bitterness, the glories, and the confusions of the new urban age seemed to find symbolic expression in Chicago. The Haymarket riot and the Pullman strike mirrored hundreds of similar clashes between labor and capital all over the country. The world's Columbian Exposition, in 1893, with its pseudo-classical architecture literally plastered on steel framework, represented both the technical competence and cultural uncertainty of the nation. When John Dewey started a laboratory school he did so in Chicago. When Theodore Dreiser described the demoralizing effects of city life Chicago was the setting. When Upton Sinclair denounced capitalism, he chose the Chicago stockyards and packing houses as his scene. Frederick Jackson Turner first presented the most influential statement of America's quest for her own identity, the frontier thesis, in Chicago.

No one can say precisely why this city captured the imagination of the nation at just this time. The spirit of the age needed a metropolis for its expression, and perhaps Chicago's newness and nearness to its frontier origins created a city where tensions and strivings were not hidden by traditions. All the currents of reform could be watched in this laboratory on Lake Michigan—the class consciousness of Samuel Gompers, the attempts by Jane Addams to eliminate class consciousness, and the reforms proposed by men who were hardly aware that class conflict even existed. Jane Addams may have pined occasionally for the simpler society of Cedarville, but her proposals looked toward bold, new departures in personal relations, ethics, and government. Samuel Gompers, while not a revolutionary, tried to bring about change as rapidly as he could. As we shall see, Robert M. La Follette and Albert Beveridge, though in fundamental disagreement on many issues, shared the view that many facets of American life needed to be changed. There was also a portion of the reform movement which devoted itself to preserving and recreating rather than experimenting and innovating. The Civic Federation of Chicago was a reform organization with these goals. Like reform-minded businessmen in New York, Philadelphia, Memphis, San Francisco, and other cities, the leaders of the Civic Federation of Chicago were men of the highest ideals and civic patriotism, yet they concentrated on issues which seemed entirely peripheral to such reformers as Robert La Follette or Jane Addams.[1] They had a short list of ills to correct, and their methods of correcting them were mild and unimaginative.

The Federation began as part of the shocked reaction to the depression of 1893. If one had to live through depression in the United States, Chicago was, after New York, the worst place in the country to do it. From every state in the Union and every country in Europe, people had been pouring into Chicago. Around the central business district an arc of slums grew up where families were crowded one on top of the other, where tenements were built in the yards of other tenements, and where light and air frequently lost the battle to soot and filth. In prosperous times people found work in the packing houses and manufacturing plants of the burgeoning city, and those out of work could turn to their church or their alderman for relief. When, early in 1893, manufacturers found their markets disappearing, scores, then hundreds, and finally thousands upon thousands of men, women, and children lost their jobs. By the fall most charity organizations had exhausted their resources. Jane Addams, who had not intended Hull House to be a charitable organization at all, found more and more of her time and money diverted into relief, and Samuel Gompers, that ardent spokesman for laissez-faire, called upon the federal government to alleviate the distress. And still the number of unemployed grew.

William T. Stead visited Chicago that fall. The editor of the English *Review of Reviews,* he had ghost written General William Booth's *In Darkest England* and was soon to write *If Christ Came to Chicago.* A Christian humanitarian, Stead was a ubiquitous reformer on both sides of the Atlantic, turning up to write a pamphlet or speak at a mass meeting whether in Chicago, New York, London, or Edinburgh. With the aid of Chicago's labor leaders, he and a group of Chicago businessmen called a meeting to consider the unployment problem. The organization of the Civic Federation of Chicago quickly followed.[2]

Organized to influence all Chicago, the Federation had a council of one hundred men elected by the incorporators, and thirty-four ward presidents. In some cases the formal structure extended even to the precinct level. The Federation divided its responsibilities among six departments: the Philanthropic Department to provide relief for the unemployed; the Industrial Department to deal with labor problems; the Municipal Department to promote clean streets and civic beauty; the Education Department to watch over the safety and adequacy of the school buildings; the Morals Department to conduct crusades against gambling; and the Political Department to bring honesty into city elections.[3]

With this complex and elaborate organization, the Federation hoped "to gather together . . . all the forces for good, public and private, which are at work in Chicago." This could be accomplished through

> the quickening of the public conscience, the arousing of the citizens to their duties and rights as citizens, the harmonizing of public and private agencies for good, the encouragement of wise and judicious legislation, the upholding of law and order, peace and justice, the

promotion of fair dealing between man and man in the industrial world, the forwarding of humane and enlightened views and practice in dealings with the unfortunate, the vicious and the defective, the advancement of the education of the masses, the ultimate separation of municipal affairs from party politics, security and honesty in elections, systematic and intelligent charity organizations, the securing of capable and interested public officials.[4]

The initial task of the Federation was relief for the unemployed. The Philanthropic Department conducted a survey of those men out of work or likely soon to be so. Applicants for aid were presented with an elaborate questionnaire asking for information on their age, marital status, country of origin, and much more. The answers were carefully tabulated, preserved, and never again referred to.[5]

Opposing the dole on the grounds that "food and lodging should be given to tramps only in return for work," the Federation developed an extensive system of work relief. As in all depressions, the unskilled needed help most, so the Philanthropic Department decided that street cleaning would provide the most appropriate employment. Gangs of men were set to work on the city streets and paid in scrip redeemable at Federation supply centers for food, clothing, and shelter. At one time the Federation was supplying aid to 3,760 men, and over a three-month period in the worst of the winter, the Federation served nearly half-a-million meals and distributed thousands of pairs of shoes, socks, and mittens, suits of underwear, and one "electric stocking." The cash outlays for this program totaled nearly ten thousand dollars, all of which was raised by private subscription.[6]

Through its employment service, the Federation hoped to move men from the street cleaning project into regular jobs. When a man left for a permanent job he received a small card which said on one side, "Good character and earnest endeavor will win the battle of life, especially in this free country, where there is generally work for all." The other side bore the legend "competent reliable men can get to the front."[7]

To men who had neither won the battle of life nor got to the front, such aphorisms may not have evoked the gratitude which the Federation intended.

Civic reformers looked upon the unemployment emergency as a temporary phenomena, but they took no such view of political corruption. Indeed, they knew that most Chicagoans accepted the bribing of aldermen as a permanent condition of civic life. All too often meetings of the city council resembled a riot rather than a dignified legislative deliberation.[8] In 1894, the Political Department hired lawyers and detectives to try to clean up at least one election. As a result, the Department obtained fifty indictments and twenty-one convictions for election fraud. Maintaining the eternal vigilance needed in Chicago, the Political Department prepared for the 1895 spring election by holding ward meetings urging people to vote in the primaries, distributing sample ballots, and endorsing honest candidates. These efforts actually defeated some of the worst candidates. By 1896 the bitterness of national politics infected local elections, and the members of the Federation found themselves unable to agree on candidates or issues. Instead of participating in the election directly, the Federation encouraged the formation of a separate organization, the Municipal Voters' League, which carried on the work of the Political Department, but with neither the endorsement nor the personnel of the Federation.[9]

Elections in Chicago were dishonest through the connivance of avaricious politicians with avaricious businessmen. The aldermen prospered on graft while the businessmen prospered on favors granted by the city council. Municipal franchises, especially for street railways provided much profit for both. As the city expanded in area, municipal services, including transportation, had to expand too. The city rather than the state assumed control over such services in 1870, but rarely exercised power, for the railways operated on city streets with their only obligation being maintenance of the streets over which their tracks ran. How much should a man pay to ride from his home to his job? How frequently ought cars to run? What safety devices ought to be on the cars? Should the railways pay the city for the monopoly privileges they enjoyed? All these questions could have been firmly answered by the city council. Instead the council allowed the lines to run where and when they would, charge what they wanted, and pay the city nothing. The most prominent of the railway operators was Charles T. Yerkes who built a financial empire based largely on overpaid construction companies, watered stock, and high fares. Yerkes avoided the threat of city regulation by buying the support of a majority of the aldermen. Sometimes he even bought the mayor himself.

In 1894, the Civic Federation recognized the "paramount responsibility" of the "obtrusion of its personality between the people and the corporations which in every city of the United States are seeking to prey on it." Election reform could help eliminate the "grey wolves," as the bought or buyable aldermen were called. In 1898, and again in 1901, the Federation attacked the traction companies directly by making comprehensive surveys of all the lines. These reports dealt almost entirely with the financing of the street railways and particularly with the value of their securities, income, expenses, return on investment, and physical assets. The reports concluded that the common stock was mostly water and that if all the water were squeezed out the lines could pay 20 per cent of their gross receipts to the city and still return 6 per cent on all bona fide capital investments. Both reports opposed municipal ownership on the grounds that service could be obtained more cheaply from private lines.[10]

The Federation achieved most of its objectives on franchise regulation and election reform. By the turn of the century Yerkes had lost his influence both in the city council and in the legislature in Springfield. The laws which were to have given him long-term rights in the city went down to defeat, along with the officials who had supported them. Chicago's elections were, for a time, more honest than they had been.

Chicago's steady expansion led not only to problems in regulating municipal services, but also to problems of governmental structure. As the city expanded by incorporating neighboring communities, the annexed towns retained some of their functions and continued to employ clerks, assessors, and other minor officials. The Federation found that duplication of duties, overlapping jurisdictions, and inequitable tax assessments made this system both unfair and inefficient. The Municipal Department drew up a series of proposals to eliminate these inefficiencies, basic to which was a new charter for the city which would streamline the government, and allow greater bonded indebtedness. From 1902 to 1907 the New Charter Movement was the chief interest of the Federation.[11]

Since the Constitution of Illinois prohibited charters for individual cities, the Federation was forced to recommend a constitutional amendment. Beginning in 1902 a committee made up of members of the Civic Federation, the Citizens Association, the Chicago Federation of Labor, the Municipal Voters' League, and Mayor Carter Harrison began the long struggle of securing enabling legislation, submitting amendments to referendum, and finally drawing up a new city charter. After five years of work the New Charter Committee submitted the charter to Chicago voters who rejected it.[12]

One purpose of the new charter was to increase Chicago's permitted bonded indebtedness and thus remove the burden of capital outlays from current tax receipts. The Civic Federation also proposed changes in the city's tax structure. Sixty to eighty per cent of Illinois' tax receipts came from what was known as the "general property tax." Based on all property, including realty, credits, personal goods, livestock, mortgages, and securities, it necessarily depended on self-assessment and thereby invited fraud. Even realty, which was officially assessed, was not assessed uniformly. After extensive studies of other cities and states, the Federation concluded that the general property tax put too much emphasis on realty, that a tax on mortgages was simply a second tax on realty, that the income tax was both difficult to administer and inquisitorial, and that an inheritance tax would be inadequate.

As a solution, the Federation proposed a clear-cut separation of the state and local tax bases. Under this plan, the state was to seek the revenue it needed from a tax on corporations, and municipalities were to derive their income from a tax on realty. Property within any community was to be assessed according to a uniform system, and revenue produced by the tax on realty was to stay in the local community. Time and again the voters of Illinois rejected the Federation's proposals; no change in the tax system was made until after World War I.[18]

By participating in the battles for clean and efficient government the Civic Federation was operating within the broad stream of reform which reached back to the Liberal Republicans of 1872 and the civil service reformers ever since. By the end of the century, many reformers asked not only that government be honest and efficient, but also more directly responsive to the popular will. As part of this widespread demand, the initiative and referendum had been adopted in several states, and had achieved a considerable momentum by the time the issue arose in Illinois in 1910. Nevertheless, after some internal differences of opinion, the Federation came out in opposition to "I & R" by calling a large opposition meeting early in 1911. At this meeting speakers from states which had recently adopted I & R damned the measures by stressing the foolishness of the electorate, the irresponsibility of giving Illinois voters more power, and the need for strong leadership as a check on popular will. Democracy and monarchy alike were condemned as despotic, and representative government was praised. Henry M. Byllesby, president of the Federation, called the proposals "attacks upon existing laws and standards," "new and untried methods" for determining public policy. More specifically the Federation opposed the I & R proposal because

1. It strikes at representative government and efficient popular control.
2. It is not progress, but a return to "town meeting"

and "mob rule," the rock on which early popular government was wrecked.

3. It doesn't cure corruption and opens the way for new graft.
4. It takes responsibility from the elected legislators and gives it to unofficial irresponsible minorities.
5. It robs the people of the opportunity for deliberate judgment.
6. It has been used as a weapon of industrial warfare.
7. It foists bad measures on the people.
8. The ballot becomes too cluttered for good judgment.[14]

These six programs—unemployment relief, electoral reform, franchise reform, tax reform, the New Charter Movement, and opposition to the initiative and referendum—constituted the bulk of the Federation's activity between its founding and 1912. During these years the organization also worked for shorter periods of time on various other projects. In 1894 the Morals Department tried to suppress gambling, first by publicizing its extent, then by raiding the gambling houses with hired detectives. In 1895, the Federation issued a call for a conference on civil service reform, and participated in the conference the following year. At various times committees of the Federation briefly investigated meat-packing houses, milk-processing plants, and bakeries, paid cursory attention to problems of industrial safety, and opposed hasty naturalization of immigrants for political purposes. The Federation demonstrated that the city's streets could be cleaned more cheaply than had been the case, and waged brief, widely scattered campaigns for the proper feeding of babies, improvements in the probation and parole system, adoption of a six-man jury system, and creation of a legal bureau in the police department.[15]

Where Jane Addams thought men were naturally both benign and capable of making wise decisions, and Samuel Gompers, while he did not think men benign, did consider them capable, the Civic Federation believed that the common run of humanity was not capable of governing itself. In opposing the initiative and referendum, the Federation insisted that direct, popular control could lead only to disaster, that the "mob" needed to be controlled, and that a more capable elite, presumably of wealth, had to lead in order to protect the people from their own foolishness.

This opinion seemed to grow out of the class attitude of the members of the Federation. Except in extreme emergencies like the depression of 1894, the Federation demonstrated little awareness of the working class, and what awareness it had was colored by hostility. At the mass meeting at which the Federation was formed, Thomas J. Morgan, a socialist leader, appealed for social justice as the only way to forestall violence. In an attempt to shake the bankers, merchants, and businessmen in the audience out of their security, Morgan ended his speech with a passionate reference to the dynamite which might explode in Chicago should justice be deferred. At his reference to violence, Morgan's audience began to mutter. As he closed his peroration shouts of protest and opposition came from all parts of the hall, some of the audience standing on their seats waving their fists at the speaker. There were references to anarchists and the Haymarket riot, a decade earlier. The meeting was saved from total disruption only by Graham Taylor, the next speaker, appealing for calmness and self-control. On the question of labor violence, those who formed the Federation were so touchy that the mere mention of dynamite caused a near riot. The point of Morgan's speech: that dissatisfaction existed and must be dealt with, was simply lost on his audience.[16]

The Federation originally conceived of itself as representing all segments of Chicago society, and chose a collective figurehead to symbolize this universality. The labor representative appears only once on the Federation records, then was never heard from again. After a brief token recognition, the Federation functioned apart from labor.

Yet labor problems were not completely ignored. In the spring of 1894 there occurred in Chicago one of the most bitter strikes in the history of American labor. The Pullman strike led the Federation to propose arbitration, a position reaffirmed at a conference on industrial relations which the Federation called in the fall of 1894. By 1902 the Federation had concluded that labor disputes should be settled by compulsory arbitration, a position bitterly opposed by all labor leaders.[17]

For the next sixteen years there was no mention of any problem connected with the working class in any Federation publication, and as early as 1911 the Federation had taken a clearly anti-labor stance. It argued that since "labor lobbyists, radicals from Toledo and Chicago radicals" favored the initiative and referendum, the proposed reforms were automatically bad. The biennial report for 1910–1911 included a generally worded but nonetheless explicit attack on labor including opposition to strikes, boycotts, picketing, and militancy in general.[18]

The members of the Federation believed that any intelligent, hard-working person could move up the economic ladder; competent, reliable men could get to the front. No artificial device, such as a strike, should be used, therefore, to facilitate this ascent. By the same token, members of the Federation assumed that the "unfortunate"—those who did not get ahead—were inherently "vicious and defective." Though these views were never stated explicitly, they were implicit in much of the Federation's work and particularly in its programs for the relief of the needy.

Along with Samuel Gompers, the Civic Federation thought of society as being divided into two polar groups. But where Samuel Gompers thought in terms of "workers" and "capitalists," the Civic Federation thought of those who mattered, and had ability and wealth; and those who mattered only when they were on the verge of starvation. The members of the Federation believed that society was governed by natural law and that everyone would automatically find his natural level. Thus the attainment of success proved ability, and poverty indicated incompetence. Clearly, public policy should be controlled by the able rather than by the incompetent.

In this society, very little needed changing. Since government (like banks and insurance companies) had a function to perform, it should be honest, efficient, and orderly. Federation members could not accept the Jane Addams view of government as a collective conscience. Rather, these men saw close connections between the virtues of order, honesty, and economy, and the greatest of these was economy. They opposed Yerkes not only because he bribed aldermen, but also because his activities increased the tax rate. The Federation did not suggest that Yerkes' lines should perform better or charge less, but that they should pay more to the city and therefore reduce the burdens on other taxpayers. Likewise, the New Charter movement had twin goals of system and economy. The charter would have systematized local government, but the Federation's chief argument was that it would reduce taxes.[19]

Honesty, system, and economy were to be achieved through publicity. Arouse the public conscience and virtue would triumph. If publicity alone were not enough, personnel, organization, or laws could be changed and evil would vanish. Thus better aldermen, a new charter, or a new franchise law could cure Chicago's ills. The Federation envisioned a good life which was not very different from life as it already was. All aldermen would be honest, election fraud would disappear, government would be simple and cheap, and public-service franchises would be granted only in return for a fair payment to the city. Private property, the class system, the industrial system, representative government, all could remain as they were. Labor lobbyists and radicals threatened changes which would bring havoc. Moreover, the Federation never looked very far for the causes of even those social ills which it did recognize. Why were so many men unemployed in 1893–1894? Why was labor becoming restive?

These questions never engaged the attention of the Federation.[20]

Perhaps the emphasis of the Civic Federation can be explained on the basis of personnel. Largely drawn from the ranks of successful businessmen, the members of the Federation were more interested in questions of taxation and administration than in the social problems of city life. Much has been made of the middle-class origins of the Progressives. Indeed, the Progressive movement has been pictured as a protest by the *petite bourgeoisie* against the malefactors of great wealth. The leadership of the Federation indicates that a wealthier group could participate in reform, and not out of a sense of *noblesse oblige,* but from pure economic self-interest.

The early presidents of the Federation were all men of considerable substance. They included Lyman J. Gage (1893–1895). Primarily a banker, he became president of the National City Bank in 1894, had organized the Chicago World's Fair in 1893, and later became Secretary of the Treasury under William McKinley and Theodore Roosevelt. William T. Baker (1895–1896) was a retired grain merchant who, at the time of the founding of the Federation, was president of the Chicago Board of Trade. Adolph Nathan (1896–1897) was a banker and investor in telephone securities. Josiah Lombard (1897–1898) was president of the Security Title and Trust Company. Franklin H. Head (1898–1900) was, besides a banker, a director of numerous Chicago corporations. La Verne W. Noyes (1900–1902) was also a banker as well as a director of an insurance company and president of a firm which manufactured windmills. Bernard E. Sunny (1902–1905) was western manager for the General Electric Corporation. Alexander H. Revell (1905–1906) was a banker and trustee of Northwestern University. John P. Byrne (1906–1907) was secretary of the Lyon and Healy Music Corporation. Clayton Mark (1907–1909, 1920–1932) was a director of the National Malleable and other Chicago iron companies as well as a director of an insurance firm. Henry

M. Byllesby (1909–1913) was an electrical engineer, an associate of Thomas A. Edison, and a director of several electric companies.

If one goes behind the presidents of the Federation to examine the occupations of the other officers, a similar pattern emerges. In 1905 and 1911, to pick sample years, the officers were: Alexander H. Revell, John P. Byrne, Frederic Greely, Joseph E. Otis, W. H. Brown, La Verne W. Noyes, Bernard E. Sunny, Adolph Nathan, E. Allen Frost, and Howard W. Sprogle for 1905; in 1911 they were Henry M. Byllesby, Joseph H. Defries, Joseph E. Otis, Douglas Sutherland, Frederick Bode, Thomas E. Donnelley, E. Allen Frost, Clayton Mark, and Adolph Nathan.

Excepting those already mention, Frederick Greely was an engineer; Joseph E. Otis was the president of the Trust and Savings bank, a real estate dealer, stock broker, and a director of tin plating and life insurance firms; William E. Brown was a highly successful real-estate dealer; E. Allen Frost, Joseph H. Defries, and Howard W. Sprogle were lawyers; Frost and Defries were also corporation directors and financiers; Joseph E. Otis was involved in tin plating and was president of what became the Central Trust Company of Illinois; Douglas Sutherland was a newspaperman of inherited wealth who devoted much of his time to civic reform; and Frederick Bode was president of a wholesale millinery company.[21]

One is hard put to find among these wealthy corporation directors, bankers, and businessmen much evidence of a *petite bourgeoisie* struggling for lost social position. If they felt irked at Charles T. Yerkes' style of living, they did not indicate it. Actually, the first and only honorary president of the Federation, Mrs. Potter Palmer, lived in a house as lavish and, if possible, uglier than Yerkes'.

The greatest gap in the Federation's reform efforts was its failure to deal with the human misery from which so many of Chicago's residents suffered. As a consequence, Jane Addams, though a founding member of the Federation, soon lost interest in the organization. In her view, the Federation's preoccupation with governmental problems left other and more pressing problems of urban life untouched.

One might actually argue that by emphasizing clean government, these reformers increased some of the worst problems of city life. In many ways the boss system, no matter how corrupt, made hard times bearable in the slums through the operation of an informal relief program. Jane Addams recognized this when she abandoned her efforts to defeat Alderman Johnny Powers. Powers had won because he was good to his constituents and filled a social need. William Lorimer, "Bath House" John Coughlin, and "Hinky Dink" Michael Kenna, all Chicago politicians of unsavory reputation, preserved their power in the same way. Carter Harrison, Jr., jeered at civil-service reformers who, with three square meals a day, tried to eliminate the graft which was Harrison's private relief system. Bosses throughout the country maintained their power by padding the roughest edges of city life. The padding was not honest but the alternative proposed by the Civic Federation was no padding at all.[22]

The Civic Federation of Chicago, widely hailed as an organization which had a "corner on virtue" and as the agent for a civic revival in Chicago,[23] occupied the right wing of the reform movement. The organization wanted change, but change which was relatively modest and narrowly confined. The Federation concerned itself with problems of government, not society. Its assumptions were essentially conservative. It distrusted both the abilities of the masses of mankind and major social change. The reforms which the Civic Federation suggested were designed to produce orderly government and social stability.

Where Jane Addams wanted social unity, and Gompers worked for social progress through class competition, the Civic Federation sought social stability and order through rule by the enlightened few. Most of the members of the Federation remained political conservatives, but some few drew implications from this doctrine which drove them toward Theodore Roosevelt's New Nationalism, itself based partly on a quest for social order through enlightened centralism. However, the New Nationalism sought these goals along paths far more radical than those followed by the Civic Federation.

4

REFORM AND POWER

Albert J. Beveridge

As a spokesman for the New Nationalism, Albert J. Beveridge marched for a while in the army of reform, but his destination was neither social unity, victory in class war, nor a comfortable and efficient *status quo.* His goal was a society more rigorously controlled and organized than that envisioned by any of the other reformers considered in these pages, and his path was determined by personal ambition and political expediency. Like Theodore Roosevelt, Beveridge came to reform through politics not principle, but unlike Roosevelt, Beveridge's political opportunism was not tempered by a fierce righteousness and a sense of *noblesse oblige.*

Beveridge's background bred an eye for the main chance and a strong sense of struggling against obstacles, rather than *noblesse oblige.*[1] When Beveridge was five years old his family plunged from moderate prosperity into poverty. His father, perhaps embittered, demanded great exertions from himself and his son to recoup lost fortune. One project involved cutting railroad-tie timber. In 1877, at the age of only fifteen, Albert went into the woods to supervise the logging. By working hard, by shouting and swearing, the lad won the respect of the loggers—or at least sufficient respect to get the logging done.

During his early years he attended school with enough regularity to have hopes of going to college. Without the money to pay for higher education, he took the examination for West Point, but failed to win admission by a fraction of a point. He thought he would have to give up college, then, as if from heaven, a wealthy citizen of Sullivan, Illinois, where Beveridge's family was living at the time, offered him fifty dollars. At least he could begin college.

When he arrived at Greencastle, Indiana, the seat of Asbury (soon DePauw) University, he found himself unable to enter even the Freshman class because he knew neither Latin nor Greek. Like Robert M. La Follette, Beveridge had to spend some weeks in a preparatory school to meet requirements in the classical languages. As a student with scanty preparation he had to spend a great deal of time on his studies. As a student with scanty finances, he had to spend a great deal of time earning his keep. As a result he slept little and budgeted his time as carefully as his money.

Beveridge's father had taught him the stern precepts of hard work and serious purpose. The lad absorbed the lessons and improved upon them. Within a few months he organized and assumed the management of a fraternity boardinghouse. At the beginning of his second year he found a better way of earning his living—entering oratorical contests. Like William Jennings Bryan and Robert M. La Follette, Beveridge found his way into politics by this route. He had a gift for putting words together and delivering them with force and conviction. In print the speeches look flowery, redundant, and often vapid, but the handsome young man with his clear voice had a natural ability to carry an audience. After his second year in college, his oratory, supplemented by a summer job as a book salesman, paid his expenses.

He drove himself too hard, however, for after graduation his health broke. Following the advice of a doctor, he went west to recuperate. But Beveridge's idea of recuperation included a venture into a potentially profitable Kansas real-estate scheme.

Wealth in Kansas was not Beveridge's long-range aim. He returned to Indiana and in 1886 began reading law in the offices of two prominent Indianapolis law partners. Again, through intellectual ability and very hard work, he quickly passed his bar exam and became something of a junior partner in his mentors' firm. Soon he was one of the most sought-after young lawyers in the state.

Beveridge's political rise, once it really engaged his attention, was as meteoric as his legal one. In the 1880's and 1890's he made many speeches for the Republican party. They were standard for the period, emphasizing Republican prosperity and waving the bloody shirt. His oratorical talent made him an effective preacher of this gospel, and he received speaking engagements of increasing importance. With the outbreak of the Spanish-American war, all his hopes and ambitions seemed to come into focus:

> For the first time in my life, I wish I were in public life. The great day of which I have, since my boyhood, been dreaming is nearly upon us. . . . I would rather take part in organizing our colonial system than anything else on this earth. I would rather map out and advocate the imperial policy of the Republic than to have been the leading statesman of the late war. It means more to humanity, more for our country and a larger place in history.[2]

Beveridge waged a short campaign, won party endorsement, and was elected United States Senator in 1898.

Here was a man whose every joust with life had ended not merely in victory but in triumph. With nearly no money he had had the temerity to enter college, with successful results. In Kansas, money and position seemed to hurry toward him. In the law, he had flashed by men twice his age with twice his experience. Now with one bound he had reached the Senate of the United States. Is it any wonder that such a life should reinforce ambition?

Once elected, Beveridge decided to see for himself the war which had so inspired him. He toured the Philippines returning only in time to take his seat in the Congress which was to consider the course of the nation in the wake of this crucial little war. Since he had spoken to nearly every important person in the Philippines, he saw no reason why he could not have the chairmanship of the committee which was to consider imperialism. Senate tradition did not allow a freshman senator a committee chairmanship, but he did get a place on the committee. Again disregarding Senate tradition, he decided he could not remain silent for the prescribed year. He gathered a voluminous amount of material and made his "Philippine Speech" in favor of imperialism. The country responded with enthusiasm, but his colleagues did not. They hazed him as mercilessly as any college freshman has ever been hazed. He responded with a "flash of silence" which won him back into senatorial good graces.

In the Senate, Beveridge turned his attention first to consolidating America's imperial position, then to the admission of the new states of Arizona and New Mexico. Only during his second term did he become clearly identified with the Progressive bloc. He introduced and fought hard for a long list of Progressive measures including railroad and corporation regulation, elimination of child labor, inspection of food, and tariff reduction. A vigorous and important member of the La Follette insurgents, he often carried much of the speaking load on the floor for that group. He was defeated in the election of 1910, never again to win public office. However, he remained a vigorous Progressive and delivered the keynote address at the Bull Moose convention of 1912.

Beveridge based his social philosophy on three fundamental attitudes, none of which necessarily implied a devotion to social change. He believed that the destiny of each of the different races of mankind was a matter of blood consciousness; he respected power in society; and he advocated the preservation of social order. Power, order, and race consciousness, when coupled with an ego of constantly expanding proportions, led Beveridge into reform.

Along with many other men of the late nineteenth century, Beveridge believed that the ultimate force in human society was a collective soul in each race which harbored an irresistible drive in a certain direction. "The key to my speech was racial," he wrote in 1900. "I consider conventional ethics and conventional morals man-made and therefore finite as of absolutely no moment compared to the higher and enduring ethic of our race."[3]

When Beveridge used the term "our race" he generally meant the Anglo-Saxon race which had produced the great explorers of Elizabethan days whose "blood within them commanded them" to seek out far lands. "Their racial tendency is as resistless as the currents of the sea. . . ." "God has not been preparing the English-speaking and Teutonic people for a thousand years for nothing but vain and idle self-contemplation and self-admiration. No! He has made us the master organizers of the world." The Anglo-Saxon race, congenitally self-governing, possessed an "institutional law with its roots springing from the very soul of our race."[4]

Americans and Canadians partook directly of this racial heritage. Close behind them were the Germans. Southern and eastern Europeans were slightly lower on the ladder of racial virtue, though Beveridge had considerable regard for the Slavs, and Asiatics occupied the lowest rung. An Oriental was capable of neither refinement nor education. The Chinese, for example, had deep character faults, the most important of which was too much regard for self and family and not enough for the community, while the Filipinos were like children, and needed the guiding hand of Anglo-Saxons. The Indiana senator seemed unaware of the existence of Negroes.[5]

Sometimes Beveridge's racism seemed to demand a rigid separation of the races. In defending colonial status for the Philippines, he argued that the "prospect of Puerto Rican, Filipino and Hawaiian Senators and Congressmen, which is the ultimate conclusion of the argument of the Constitution extending over these possessions, is not a spectacle to be viewed calmly." In Asiatic Russia where he saw many races mingling freely, he said that Anglo-Saxons were naturally startled by such racial harmony. Later, however, when arguing for a unified state of Arizona and New Mexico, he emphasized the easy amalgamation of Spanish and American blood and gave racial mixing high credit for producing America's greatness.[6]

Beveridge felt that the peculiar greatness of the Anglo-Saxon race lay in its ability to create social order, perhaps the most important of Beveridge's social goals. Where Samuel Gompers and Jane Addams demanded social justice, Beveridge insisted on order. Liberty was for Beveridge "realized only by him who obeys those common rules of action called laws by which alone liberty lives." Civilization meant "liberty and law . . . social order and the Gospel of our Lord." He praised the Puritans because order was for them "as necessary as honesty; law as essential as liberty; government as important as resistance to wrong." Cardinal Richelieu, Edmund Burke, and George Washington were great not because of their wisdom or vision but because all three had brought order out of chaos. Beveridge regarded the French Revolution not as a triumph of democracy but as a catastrophe, because it led to violence. The need for order was another reason why the United States should keep the Philippines: the natives "like all backward peoples need to be taught orderly continuous labor before anything else."[7]

Beveridge's desire for order, even before justice, was most strikingly illustrated by his reaction to tsarist Russia. On his journey through Manchuria in 1902, he saw Russian methods of colonization. He was favorably impressed by the Russians' swift justice and praised them for killing three thousand robbers in six weeks. Since the Russians brought order out of chaos, he justified their brutal methods.

Social order could be achieved only through the use of power, the third in Beveridge's trinity of values. Christ alone excepted, in the Bible Beveridge admired above all David and Moses, the warrior and the lawgiver, power and order. He had tremendous respect for the Russian Orthodox Church, not because of its doctrine or its moral teaching but because of the power it held over the Russian people and the fervent loyalty it inspired. Beveridge also had high praise for Sergei Witte, finance minister, who was trying to reorganize tsarist finance on European lines, and Konstantin Podebonostsev, a close advisor to the tsar and an arch reactionary, but he denounced a third Russian as an unrealistic dreamer who, if he had any effect at all upon the world, would have a bad effect. This man was a nobleman living the life of a peasant, Count Leo Tolstoy.[8]

Beveridge based his nationalism on his desire for order and his respect for power. He expounded his views most clearly in his speech on Governor John P. Altgeld's action in the Pullman strike of 1894. Over Altgeld's protest that the troops were unnecessary and their dispatch unconstitutional, President Grover Cleveland had sent in troops to quell violence. The Republican senator's speech, given at the height of the presidential campaign of 1896, supported the Democratic President.[9] Beveridge denounced Altgeld for supporting the proposition "that the general government cannot suppress red riot, extinguish the fires of arson and protect property from destruction and life from frenzy blinded mobs without the consent of the governor of the state." This Beveridge called "the principle of national decay."

The federal government represented a single people, Beveridge insisted, divided into states merely for administrative convenience. The President represented that single people. Every locality had a responsibility to the nation and must not be allowed to disrupt national affairs with local disturbances. The President had to use his power to preserve order, for "hesitation of power is the food upon which mobs grow formidable and fierce. The danger that threatens our future is local demagogues—not federal despots."[10]

As a nationalist, Beveridge praised all those who had increased the power of the central government. Thomas Jefferson as President, Andrew Jackson, George Washington, Abraham Lincoln, Theodore Roosevelt, and above all John Marshall were nation builders who deserved the thanks of the nation they wrought. Beveridge derided the doctrine of states' rights as merely a device behind which evil-doers hid for their own selfish ends. There was no danger of federal tyranny since the national government represented all of the people at once, and the states represented all the people divided into forty-six pieces. The central government could not harm the states, for that would be self-harm.[11]

Beveridge's praise for centralized power led him to approve of concentration both in labor and industry. Huge business organizations, a natural product of industrialization, brought gains in efficiency and lowered costs. Moreover Beveridge thought that dissolution of these corporations was impossible and that their occasional abuses of power could be curbed through the use of the federal police power.[12]

Similarly, labor organizations were a natural development of industrialism. Beveridge did not argue that labor had to organize in order to do battle with capital, for class conflict was not that evident to him and, as his comments on the Pullman strike indicate, he had no real understanding of the goals of organized labor. The economic system led naturally to unions which could be useful schools for self-government, mutual improvement, and self-respect. How different these purposes were from Samuel Gompers' view of labor as an army![13]

While Beveridge sought an orderly society, he did not want a static one. Change was brought about by great irresistible forces which Beveridge usually termed "destiny." One aspect of destiny was racial instinct. Another was the ineluctable process of social maturation, for in Beveridge's view societies started as children, matured, then declined into senility. Another factor was geography which, for example, was driving Russia east and Japan west, toward an inevitable clash. Geography also required the United States to expand into the Pacific and Caribbean.[14]

With Theodore Roosevelt, Beveridge believed that one of the ways in which the forces of destiny worked was through war. "We hearken not to rhymers on universal peace, for we know that with the sword the world has ever out of error

carved its good estate. . . . I subscribe to the doctrine of
war. It is the divine instrument of progress. Every lasting
victory of human freedom was won upon the field."[15] Indeed,
one important reason he opposed child labor was that it
weakened the future soldiers of the nation.

While the forces of destiny determined the direction of
social change, Beveridge agreed with La Follette that the
mechanics of change ought to be planned and worked out
by experts. This was partly an outgrowth of Beveridge's
esteem for centralized and efficient power, for he pictured
a commission of experts handing down decisions which legislators and businessmen would be expected to follow. Partly
too it was a result of his confidence in destiny, for the experts would not determine policy but merely the natural
next step in an already destined direction. He thought that
the scientific method could lead to truth in human affairs,
and he praised other countries for employing it: Canada's
conservation measures, Germany's tariff commission, the careful planning which went into the freeing of the serfs in
Russia.[16]

Beveridge's opinion of how fast social change should take
place itself changed through the years. In his first speech in
the Senate, the speech urging the United States to keep the
Philippines, Beveridge argued for a great departure from
traditional policy and insisted that the nation should not be
bound by the past. The United States should ride destiny
wherever it might go. While insisting that the Founding
Fathers had intended the nation to be imperialistic, he made
no attempt to disguise the fact that he was urging innovation. Circumstances often required the exercise of powers
not specified in the Constitution. That document was not
made to freeze American institutions as they were in 1787.
"The march of nationality is not to be withstood; and so the
salvation of the Constitution is in its capacity for growth."
"It has long been clear to me," he wrote, "that as a practical matter, no paper barrier would stand in the way of a
mighty people's development."[17]

Over the years he changed his emphasis, concentrating

more and more on the links which his proposals had with the past. Perhaps this shift had a political explanation. As he became more identified with the insurgent wing of the Republican party, he may have stressed the conservative nature of his views in order to avoid being tarred with a radical brush. As early as 1902, he was calling himself a conservative, but to him the term simply meant change without violence. By 1906 Beveridge was clearly emphasizing the conservative nature of the reforms he had supported. He contended that regulation of business must be worked out gradually in the context of changing social and economic conditions, and he insisted that laws such as the Hepburn Act (regulating railroads) and the Pure Food and Drug Act were simply natural products of a changing situation, not new social experiments.[18]

In Beveridge's list of factors which produced social change, ideas had no place. Early in his senatorial career, he said that "public policies are wise only as they express a people's development. This is why most of the plans of reformers fail, why most of the theories of dreamers are idle. They are born of some individual's thought." In spite of the fact that he later became a scholar and biographer, his contempt for theorizers and bookish men was complete. He said that about the only books of any importance were the Bible, Shakespeare's works, and the writings of Robert Burns. Going to college had a limited utility, but young men should go if they could because college would instill habits of hard work and order which would be useful later on. "The fourth quality in character," he wrote, "the lowest on the list is Intellect." Brains were abundant; successful men could hire brains. Beveridge thought that books were merely second-hand experience. First-hand experience and action were much more important. In 1898 he wrote: "As to Gladstone himself, I cannot agree with you as to his greatness. He did not 'do things', he talked. . . . Give me the men who 'do things'."[19]

Beveridge's respect for men who did things led him, during his early years in the Senate, to equate moral excellence with achievement and achievement with wealth. In 1892 he declared that "Every step toward plenty and comfort is a step toward civilization. Every step toward want and misery and endless toil is a step toward barbarism." In his speeches for the 1892, 1894, and 1896 campaigns, he consistently equated prosperity and wealth with virtue. In arguing for imperialism he insisted that commerce was a method by which the savages could be civilized. He extolled the career of Thomas R. Scott, president of the Pennsylvania Railroad, saying that Scott's life "demonstrated that the very ultimate of achieving, the very crest of effort and reward may be reached by men who know neither Latin nor Greek."[20]

About 1905, Beveridge began to damn commercial standards. Perhaps he had become disillusioned with materialism, but there is no evidence of soul searching or that he was aware of contradicting his earlier statements. In 1906 he hoped that "financial interests" would no longer be the national ideal, and by 1910 he argued that "the curse of our present day is greed. We measure everything by dollars. We worship wealth." His keynote speech at the Bull Moose convention in 1912 was interlaced with typical Progressive rhetoric against wealth.[21]

Here again, the shift in emphasis may have a political explanation. In the rising tide of Progressive sentiment in the country, Beveridge may have seen a means for the fulfillment of his own political ambitions. Perhaps most politicians aspire to the Presidency, but Beveridge seemed to think that destiny would be shirking her duty if she did not place him in the White House. His political rise had been rapid but his egotism grew even more swiftly. As a freshman senator, he fully expected a subcommittee chairmanship. He made a major policy address almost as soon as he had taken his seat. Although this speech irritated his colleagues, it received enough national attention to fire his already heated ambition.

By 1900, barely a year after he had taken his seat in the Senate, he was already envisioning himself as a successor to William McKinley. With more optimism than good judgment, he noted that "things are simply perfect here. I am in the inner inside circle." Then he spoke jubilantly of the formation of several "Beveridge for President" clubs. After he had been in public office for only eleven months he wrote to George H. Lorimer, publisher of the *Saturday Evening Post*, that his Philippine speech had received great support in the South, and that he, Beveridge, might be the man to bring some Southern strength to the Republican party. In writing of this Southern support to one of his friends he said he would be glad if he could "inspire [respect] in that finest and most unadulterated of the Anglo-Saxon race." Beveridge's self-esteem was like the simple egotism of a child who has no doubt that he is the precise center of the universe. "I have done some mighty big things over simply incredible obstacles," he wrote his friend David Graham Phillips in 1908, "and I think before you get through these ought to be recognized."[22]

This egotism and political ambition turned his ideas of race, power, and order in the direction of reform. His record was not so much one of slow growth toward Progressivism as of sudden conversion. In the 1890's, Beveridge cast his speeches in the mold of orthodox Republican oratory. He waved the bloody shirt with the best, praised prosperity and McKinley, demanded a high protective tariff, and damned the Democrats. At the turn of the century he extolled everything American, and even as late as 1904 he entitled a speech "All is Well with the Republic." It was a hymn to things as they were.[23] These sentiments stand in sharp contrast to those of Robert La Follette, who from 1892 on, saw impending doom unless basic changes were made in the nation's political and economic organization.

Suddenly, in 1906, Beveridge changed his views. Thereafter he took the Progressive side of every question. In that year he could say that the Republican party "must not stop" but must turn to "those new social and economic questions which have to do with the daily lives and happiness of human beings," and he applauded Roosevelt's endorsement of radicalism in the inheritance tax. In 1908, using language much like that of La Follette, he wrote to the President: "I dislike legislation which gives people the impression that something very much worthwhile has been done, when as a matter of fact very little has been done." In 1910 and 1911 Beveridge argued for more direct popular influence in government and insisted that business and special interests must get out of government and let the people rule. Convinced that he had lost the Senate seat in 1910 because the Republican party had not been Progressive enough, he tried to recoup his losses by continuing to advocate a bold, reform program.[24] He supported Roosevelt in 1912 and delivered the keynote speech at the Bull Moose convention endorsing woman suffrage, initiative and referendum, and a host of measures dealing with social welfare and business regulation.

No sudden awareness of social ills can account for Beveridge's changed position. He knew no more about poverty, corporate abuses, or popular government in 1906 than he had known in 1904. He did know, however, that President Roosevelt's reform measures were popular with the electorate, and he believed that his party had to follow the path of reform if it was to retain power. "The people are behind the President and want their congressmen behind [him]. They give him all the credit for the great reforms, not congress, and congress had better go along," he wrote.[25] This does not imply that Beveridge was completely hypocritical. Some degree of opportunism is vital to success in politics. More than this, in the first years of the twentieth century, Beveridge, like Theodore Roosevelt, adapted his basic social attitudes to the needs of reform. Before 1904, Beveridge, while showing no interest in reform, had shown enthusiasm for centralized, efficient, and powerful government.

One segment of reform thought, as summed up in Herbert Croly's *Promise of American Life,* found centralized power the most useful tool for social reform. Theodore Roosevelt made this ideology politically successful. It was here that

Beveridge found his political home. In another time or another place Beveridge's regard for power, order, and racial consciousness might have led him toward a policy of conservatism or even toward something approaching the fascism of Benito Mussolini. Instead, during the first decade of the twentieth century, and in the United States, he arrived at Progressivism. Beveridge was not following reform so much as his vision of a highly centralized state run by an efficient and powerful government.

5

REFORM AND THE ELITE

Edgar Gardner Murphy

As a Progressive, Albert Beveridge concentrated a large measure of his efforts on the attempt to eliminate child labor. Indeed, his approach to the problem, through the commerce power of the federal government, eventually became national policy. Several Southern reformers assisted mightily in this crusade, among them an Episcopal priest from Alabama named Edgar Gardner Murphy. Although Beveridge and Murphy saw and worked to eliminate the same evil, two men further apart in their fundamental social philosophy would be hard to imagine. Murphy shared Beveridge's strong sense of racial instinct, but when combined with the elitism of the Civic Federation of Chicago and the gentle humanitarianism of Jane Addams, the resulting ideology contrasted sharply with that espoused by the other reformers considered in these pages.

Murphy, one of those reformers in the "New South" who functioned not in politics but in the areas of race relations, education, and limitations on child labor, came to his reforms through a strong sense of Christian duty. Born in 1869 in Fort Smith, Arkansas, he was brought up in a devout Episcopalian family which was dominated by his mother and aunt, for his father had deserted when Edgar was three years old.[1] Years later Edgar remembered his "Auntie," always kneeling for family prayers, despite severe rheumatic pains. Moving to San Antonio, the two women opened a boarding house which provided an income at first adequate, then comfortable. The minister of their Episcopal church took a particular interest in young Edgar, and at an early age the boy decided to enter the ministry. No decision could have pleased his family more.

By the time Edgar was ready for college in 1884, the family finances permitted him to attend the University of the South at Sewanee, Tennessee. There he came under the influence of a professor of New Testament literature, William Porcher DuBose. DuBose and Murphy took to each other, maintaining a close, warm friendship until Murphy's death. Perhaps Professor DuBose, a scholarly, devout, and warm-hearted man, filled some of the gap caused by an absent father. After graduating in 1888 Murphy spent a year at General Theological Seminary in New York. Since he did not want to strain family finances by staying longer, he returned to San Antonio to become assistant in a large church and, now ordained, pastor of a smaller congregation. In 1891 he married Maude King, a high-school teacher in San Antonio who was originally from Massachusetts. Soon they moved to Laredo, where their first child was born. They named him DuBose, in honor of Murphy's mentor at Sewanee.

The year of the baby's birth, 1893, also saw Edgar Gardner Murphy's entrance into social action. In Paris, Texas, a Negro had been brutally beaten and lynched by an enraged mob. Shocked, Murphy refused to remain idle. He issued a call for a mass meeting in Laredo and persuaded important city officials to attend. The meeting only partially succeeded. Few citizens attended, and the vigorous resolutions which Murphy had prepared aroused little enthusiasm. Nevertheless, Murphy had begun the career of social reform which was eventually to lead him out of the church entirely.

This incident in many ways illustrates his approach to social action. His original impulse was humanitarian, growing out of his abhorrence of brutality. He sought his ends through publicity, not politics. His approach was conservative in that he made sure respected city officials would be at the meetings, and he demanded nothing more in the way of action than the expression of opinion. Yet his Christianity demanded that *some* protest be voiced against un-Christian actions.

In 1893 and 1894, the Murphy family suffered a series of illnesses. Murphy himself had had rheumatic fever as a child. He had been pronounced cured, but the ordeal had weakened his heart and in later years extended periods of intensive work were usually followed by a physical collapse, the cause of which baffled his doctors. Since the Laredo climate was hard on the whole family, he accepted positions first in Chillicothe, Ohio, then in Kingston, New York. Though their health improved in these places, Murphy was glad to receive an invitation from St. John's Church in Montgomery, Alabama, for he regarded the South as his home.

The Montgomery church provided Murphy with an assistant. Freed of the routine duties of his calling he devoted himself to local social problems, the most pressing of which was relations between the races. Following the pattern set in his reaction to the Paris lynching, he proposed a conference in Montgomery where leading Southerners, both ministers and laity, could consider race relations. Hearing of these plans, Booker T. Washington invited Murphy to attend a commencement at Tuskegee Institute. Although not officially on the program, Murphy spoke extemporaneously on the aims and methods of the conference he was organizing. His message, that Negroes had not yet been granted the full emancipation to which they were entitled, was welcome at Tuskegee. His tone, moderate and compassionate rather than militant, appealed both to Washington and to the white men in the audience. Two of these, William H. Baldwin, president of the Long Island Railroad and a trustee of Tuskegee, and Robert C. Ogden, a New York businessman and chairman of the Board of Hampton Institute, were impressed with Murphy's views. Within a few years they were to sponsor the major portion of his reform efforts, through the Southern Education Board.

The Conference on Race Problems, held in May of 1900,

led to invitations for Murphy to speak all over the East. In New York, Washington, and Boston he came into contact with the broad stream of social reform of the Progressive era. He met such influential editors as Lyman Abbott, Walter Hines Page, and Albert Shaw, as well as such philanthropists as Andrew Carnegie and George Foster Peabody. Ever alert to the needs of his home city, Murphy persuaded Carnegie to give Montgomery a library, and Peabody to donate a Y.M.C.A. building.

Almost immediately after the Conference on Race Problems, Murphy began applying his ideas to a specific issue —Alabama's plan to formalize Negro disfranchisement, a goal accomplished since Reconstruction by subterfuge. His solution was to insist on "white supremacy" by which he meant the supremacy of "property and intelligence." White men with neither, he wrote, should be disfranchised. Negroes with both should vote. The constitutional convention adopted a system of property and literacy requirements of which Murphy approved, since at least on their face, they would apply equally to both races.

That same year, 1900, Irene Ashby, an investigator for the AF of L, came to Murphy with her report on the condition of children working in Southern textile mills. Again, Murphy's humanitarian instincts were aroused, and he began to oppose child labor. This cause brought him into direct contact with other reformers such as Jane Addams and Albert Beveridge. He started out by organizing the Alabama Child Labor Committee which in 1903 secured passage of a law prohibiting the worst abuses. A year later the Alabama group joined the National Child Labor Committee with Alexander McKelway, Felix Adler, Florence Kelley, and Murphy as guiding spirits. Eventually, this committee endorsed federal regulation of child labor, but Murphy retained so much emotional sympathy for the traditional Southern states-rights view that he chose to resign from the committee rather than endorse this extension of federal power.

Murphy not only wanted to get children out of factories,

he wanted to get them into schools. The improvement of Southern education was the cause closest to his heart. His friend from Tuskegee, Robert C. Ogden, had conceived the idea of a private group to improve education all over the nation. He wanted Murphy to participate by setting up and running the Southern Education Board. Financed by Ogden and his friends, including John D. Rockefeller, the board proposed to rouse the South to the need for more and better schools. Murphy's chief task was to build and maintain enthusiasm through annual conferences.

By 1903 Murphy felt that his involvement in reform prevented him from carrying on as a minister. He had resigned from his post at St. John's two years before, and now felt that he should leave the ministry altogether. This was not only a matter of other pressing demands on his time. He felt that he would be respected more as an equal if he were a layman. He continued his work for racial harmony, control of child labor, and improved education until 1909, when his rapidly deteriorating health forced him to resign all his duties. He lived only four more years.

Edgar Gardner Murphy's trinity of reforms focused on his section's most pressing problems during the period when the South struggled to overcome the political instability left by Civil War and Reconstruction. Until the mid-1870's political alignments had been strongly influenced by the presence of federal troops and the whole apparatus of the Reconstruction effort. When this structure was dismantled, very little was available to take its place. Prewar political loyalties had been destroyed or had become irrelevant. Nominally, only one party, the Democratic, remained in the South, and within it faction strove with faction for political control. One group, predominantly prewar Whigs who now called themselves Democrats, wanted to "redeem" the South through the development of railroads and industry. As former planters, many of these men had considerable influence over the Negro vote. Another faction, often called Independents and made up largely of poor, back-country farmers, wanted not so much to control as to eliminate the Negro vote. Under various names, this division along class and partly geographical lines, was the basis for Southern politics until the Woodrow Wilson movement of 1910.

The gradual withdrawal of federal troops generally left the Democratic party in the hands of the more conservative "Redeemers." The back country "Independents," since they could not become Republicans, gravitated to such new organizations as the Southern Alliance, then to the Populist party. Starting with demands for economic relief through railroad regulation, co-operative marketing, and easier credit, this group soon broadened its program to include such political measures as the direct primary, the initiative, referendum, and recall. Southern Populism combined economic necessity and political conviction with an attempt to wrest control of the Democratic party from the more conservative elements.

With the rise of these small farmers, rednecks as they came to be called, went a decline in the position of the Negro. In the South of the 'nineties, political democracy and racism grew out of the same mechanism and drew their support from the same groups. The Alliance men and Populists worked alongside and competed with Negroes. Their economic interest might have bound them together, but, after the mid-'nineties, it did not. Just as the poor whites had favored slavery as a sure sign that they were at least one rung up the social and economic ladder, so the rednecks welcomed Jim Crow because it prevented social leveling with Negroes.

Racial discrimination, then, was not so much a product of the end of Reconstruction as it was of the power struggle of the 'nineties in which the redneck element gained increasing influence. Railroad cars, restaurants, and drinking fountains, which had served both races, now became segregated. The disfranchisement of Negro voters, the inevitable climax of discrimination, began in Mississippi in 1890 and soon spread to all Southern states.

Meanwhile, the conservatives had not been idle. They

condemned the Alliance and Populism for disrupting the only party which could protect the South and for destroying connections with eastern wealth in favor of links with mid-western radicalism. These conservative, old-line Whigs heaped scorn on the new leaders who won political power through demogoguery rather than proven political ability, and though these conservatives accepted Negro disfranchisement, they thought that logic and common sense demanded that the most ignorant whites should be barred from voting as well. They saw Southern salvation coming from increased industrialism, extended urbanization, and improved education; they abhorred the mobocracy of the rednecks.

Conservative only in that they opposed the hegemony of semi-literate small farmers, the old-line Whigs wanted neither to stand pat nor to return to ante-bellum days. Most started not from politics, a sphere over which they exercised less and less control, but from social affairs, and they often worked through private philanthropic organizations. They concentrated their reform efforts on race relations, child labor, and education, and approached each without the tumult and shouting of the Populists. But racism, though muted, crept into their attitudes. Edgar Gardner Murphy devoted the full measure of his sometimes scanty energy to this group.

Murphy's basic reason for entering reform was an intense awareness of the misery, poverty, and ignorance which were the lot of many Southern families, especially the children. While not strictly speaking an advocate of the Social Gospel, he felt that Christians had to express themselves on the problems of the age. A man of intense conviction and firm moral rectitude, he always tempered his ardor for eliminating evil with a personal gentleness, a respect for tradition, a desire for order, and an awareness of the limited effects of his efforts. Although he participated in the most important efforts at social amelioration in the New South he was a pessimist among reformers. Not sharing the reformers' usual assumptions that men were essentially good, needing only liberation for their benignity to flourish, he believed that human instincts were malevolent, that human abilities were sharply limited, and that men needed to be restrained rather than liberated.

Sharing the environmentalism of naturalist novelists, frontier historians, and social Darwinists of all political stripes, Murphy saw the human mind inescapably imprisoned by its surroundings. He thought that agricultural labor was intellectually debilitating, that economic inequality led to racial friction, and that in general "the profounder education of men springs even more directly from the educational force of the process of production."[2] Karl Marx himself could hardly have been more explicit.

The limiting environment was partly a product of the past. For Murphy the past was not a dead hand, but a palpable, living one. All understanding of the present, he thought, must come from an appreciation of the past. In one sense this reverence for the past meant that there were aspects of society which Murphy believed could not be changed. Because of its history, the heterogenous South could not be made homogenous. In another sense his respect for the past led him to see history as a standard of moral excellence. He did not quite insist that whatever is, is right, but he did think that ideas and institutions which had withstood the test of time were probably more correct than new or temporary modes of thought and action.

His respect for the past did not lead him to counsel social immobility. As reformers must, he believed in the possibility of progress, yet he was far less sanguine than Robert La Follette or Jane Addams. While he thought that "no problem need be the occasion for discouragement so long as the problem is apparently yielding to the forces of its reduction," he used a relative word "reduction," rather than an absolute one like "solved." In fact, he said that

the great problems of life are never solved in any mathematical or final sense. They are solved only in the sense that life becomes adjusted to them, or in the sense that their conflicting or complementary elements find a working adjustment to one another, an adjustment consistent in larger and larger measure with wisdom, right, happiness; but always coincident with the possibility of misconception and with recurrent periods of acute antagonism.[4]

Yet every age demanded change. In his era, Murphy thought the times demanded a certain minimum of economic and political rights for Negroes. Even more important, the South ought to adopt the industrial system which other sections were exploiting with such success. As in the nineteenth century, northern industry had the force of destiny behind it and could not be resisted.[5]

Neither Murphy's respect for the past, nor his acknowledgement of the necessity of change allowed much room for conscious human control of events. In fact, he frequently spoke in metaphors based on simple mechanics. "Forces" acted on one another producing "reactions" and "recoils." He believed that discrimination against Negroes could not be maintained because "in the long run our political proscriptions in America are always defeated by forces deeper than those of external inhibitions."[6] With Albert J. Beveridge, Murphy believed that thought and action had to bow before these deeper forces.

Along with limitations on human abilities, Murphy held grave doubts about human benignity. Where Jane Addams saw conflict as a product of a misconstructed society, Murphy saw conflict as a natural state of the world, which society might assuage. Murphy believed that a certain amount of cohesion could exist within various groups, but antagonism and misunderstanding were natural between groups.

> It is not natural that a white man should understand a black man, or that a black man should understand a white man. The Irishman does not understand the German, nor the German the Irishman; nor have the Jews and Gentiles yet dissolved the conditions of estrangement which have divided them.[7]

Samuel Gompers similarly saw society made up of mutually

opaque groups, but where Gompers saw only two groups, Murphy saw a great multiplicity.

While Murphy wished to change important aspects of Southern society, he accepted many of the ideas endemic to his region. With urban life rapidly becoming predominant in the nation, Murphy, along with others from rural backgrounds, insisted on the virtues of the "simpler and more wholesome conditions of the country." He blamed much of the criminality of Northern Negroes on the conditions of city life. Yet, perhaps more than some others, he recognized the greater social efficiency if not the wholesomeness of urban living, and wanted to bring these efficiencies to the South.[8]

Murphy also vigorously opposed extending federal power. He thought that the Fourteenth and Fifteenth amendments were unenforceable in the South. Essentially uninterested in political rights for Negroes, he was unable to rise above his sectional devotion to doctrines of states' rights and insisted that injecting the federal government into the franchise would turn every white Southerner from being a friend of the Negro into a foe of Washington and therefore of the Negro whom Washington protected. Likewise, he vigorously opposed federal regulation of child labor, although he worked hard to keep children out of the factories. He resigned from the National Child Labor Committee because that group endorsed Senator Beveridge's bill forbidding the interstate shipment of goods produced by children. Apparently Murphy was willing to accept federal aid for reform if that aid was only financial, not proscriptive, for he thought Southern education needed financial support from the federal government. He did not want "the academic fabric of paper theories [presumably states' rights] to stand between the vast resources of the nation's wealth and the human appeal, North or South, East or West of the children of its citizenship."[9]

The question of the relationship between whites and Negroes lay at the center of the social philosophy of most

Southern reformers. But Edgar Gardner Murphy was not primarily concerned with race relations. In fact, his work on education and child labor would have been simplified had he not had the race problem to deal with. Yet Murphy believed that race was a primary, undeniable, and unalterable fact of human existence. "The deepest thing about any man —next to his humanity itself—is his race. . . . No Negro can escape, or ought to desire to escape, the Africa of his past." A congenital race consciousness in every human being could be fulfilled only if each person felt a pride in his racial heritage. This would enable American Negroes to unite around their common background when the African nations achieved political independence. Race consciousness also created a sort of racial tropism according to which members of one race preferred to be with others of the same race. Thus for Murphy, such physical characteristics as skin color merely symbolized the existence of deeper character differences between the races.[10]

The racial heritage of even the most uneducated white man provided him with a free spirit and the capacity to learn. Similarly all Poles, Slavs, and Chinese drew on a significant cultural heritage, but Negroes, thought Murphy, because their past was a void, had no reserves of culture and civilization upon which to draw. Insisting that the inherent inferiority of the Negro race was an unproven, theoretical problem, Murphy instead argued that in the United States at the beginning of the twentieth century, Negroes were "weaker" than whites. Thus social and political equality was "nonsense." While "The fact that the Negro is a Negro the state may not alter," this did not mean that improvement could not be made in the Negro's lot. "The fact that the Negro, both at the North and at the South has not been adequately accorded the economic support of the profounder social forces of security, opportunity, and hope, the State may largely alter if it will."[11]

Murphy seemed to favor two parallel civilizations in the South, one black, one white, with very little contact between them. Above all, what he called "racial fusion" had to be avoided. While he condemned racial hatred, he maintained that a mutual antipathy was both unavoidable and good, for it kept the two unmixable families of men from any close contact. He supported separation but insisted that the social wall should not enclose a ghetto; the sunshine of opportunity should shine on both sides.[12]

Murphy was sure that in the statistical aggregate, Negroes would have fewer able men than whites would, but each person's capacity ought to be judged individually. Negroes had made tremendous progress in "civilization" since they came from Africa, and there was no reason to think they could not make more. Exceptionally able Negroes ought to get an exceptional education. This would not only provide educated leadership for the race, but would give hope to ambitious Negroes. Murphy spoke of a Negro who was "industrious, sensible, self-respecting. . . . Do we want him? We do. Do we want him to stay? We do. How shall we treat him? Treat him justly. Give protection to his life and property. Give his children a chance. Let *him* vote." At the turn of the century Murphy felt that most Negroes lacked the property and education to qualify as voters, and that they should be helped toward the material and educational levels which would justify granting them the franchise. Booker T. Washington had advocated a similar solution, known as the Atlanta Compromise. Murphy preferred it to the radical and "extreme" proposals advanced by the newly formed National Association for the Advancement of Colored People.[13]

Murphy's demand for a literacy and property test as a qualification for voting was not simply a ruse to disfranchise Negroes. He recognized that large numbers of whites in every Southern state were illiterate and he did not hesitate to propose their disfranchisement. An unabashed aristocrat, Murphy feared the mob, regardless of its skin color. If there were unrestricted manhood suffrage, whether or not Negroes voted, "the congressional power of the Southern

States would rest, without possibility of escape, in the hands of its very crudest and lowest forces; threatening in Congress the dignity and peace of the Nation and imperiling at the South the fundamental securities and property as well as the large and noble policies of the States."[14]

Murphy's arguments in favor of Negro opportunity to advance materially and educationally were based partly on white self-interest and were probably sincere. "It is not a good thing for any race to be perpetually dealing with another race with which it does not have to argue . . . and for whom it may act without any real partnership in responsibility." Moreover a general moral illness developed in any person, black or white, who received less than humane treatment at the hands of his fellows. Whites could not overthrow the law as a means of repressing Negroes without at the same time destroying their own respect for the legal order; they could not cheat Negroes without spreading the cancer of immorality throughout society, black no less than white. For the self-interest of all, argued Murphy, race relations had to be based on mutual respect.[15]

Murphy practiced what he preached in his relations with Booker T. Washington. Of course, Washington was regarded as an exceptional, untypical Negro, whose program of slow progress accorded perfectly with Murphy's own ideas. While Murphy had no objection to Washington using the back stairs of a hotel, the respectful and courteous tone of his letters to Washington indicates genuine admiration.[16]

While Murphy did not envisage the eventual disappearance of racial differences, he regarded the violent friction of his day as a temporary heritage from slavery and Reconstruction, and he looked forward to a time when a new generation of Southerners would lead each race toward a feeling of respect for the other. Unless Southern whites took the initiative in bringing this about, others would force the situation on the South, a calamity for both races. The period of harmony would come more quickly if Negroes were not economically underprivileged, thus adding economic resentment to racial antipathy. Speaking of both races, he said that no man should remain bound to one class. Society gained as men advanced, and all who wanted and could benefit from training should have it.[17]

Central to Murphy's arguments in favor of enlarging opportunities for the oppressed was a fear that without them they would create social disorder. He, like Beveridge, regarded order as the basic requisite of society. Freedom, he said, in words much like those of the Indiana senator, was not "a man in a vast waste of silence sitting naked beneath a solitary tree," but was a social achievement dependent upon a well-ordered society. Government, the institution charged with the responsibility for preserving order, must possess the power necessary to fulfill its obligations, even at the cost of interfering with some theoretical rights.[18]

The opportunity to rise could best be provided by education, which was the central core of all Murphy's reform efforts. His work against child labor, for Negro rights, and on the Southern Education Board, all revolved around education. "Education," he argued, "is the process by which the irresponsible are bound into the life of the responsible, . . . by which a people is changed from a mob into a society." Education is a "task of collective consecration, the task of society and of humanity" because "the most ignorant everywhere are always the most suspicious and the most prone to class antagonisms."[19] Here Murphy pictured schools not so much as the transmitters of a received culture or as the training grounds for a vocation, but as socializing institutions, a concept vaguely similar to some of John Dewey's.

Murphy saw the rural nature of the South, knew that Southern society was changing rapidly, and thought that only through the schools could these widely scattered rural people be prepared to cope with such changes. An educational system supported by the state had a duty to train children for citizenship and democracy. This could be done through the

elimination of civic ignorance, so that more and more people would have the information and understanding which
Murphy considered essential for the vote.[20]

Education could also be the prime agent in increasing
understanding between the races, partly by allowing each
race to find out more about the other. More important, education could ease the psychological strain created in both
races by emancipation, and train young Southerners to as-
sume important governmental and business positions. Unless this were done, all political and economic power would
fall into the hands of "outsiders," a situation Murphy thought
would be calamitous.[21]

Yet Murphy was not one to grant schools a purely social
function. Education was part of that process which satisfied
the natural human need for understanding, the need for
answers to the question of how the universe worked. Within every man was a desire for certainty. Like religion, the
schools helped meet this need. In addition, education was
a liberating and stimulating process, creating new needs as
it satisfied old ones. However, these new needs were on a
higher level and involved greater sophistication and more
controlled desires. Society owed everyone the training necessary to earn a living, but education must include cultural
enrichment as well. "The end of society is not the culture of
the few. The end of culture is the enlightenment and happiness of society."[22]

While believing fervently in the efficacy of education,
Murphy was poignantly aware of its limitations and dangers.
"There is always present the danger of superficiality. . . .
Many a blind heart which was at peace in its blindness has
gained only enough light to lose its peace without the gain
of full and accurate sight. . . . But the risk of making fools
is of smaller import than the chance of making men."[23]

Murphy's belief that progress occurred as men learned
restraint led him to insist that only those men who had
learned restraint ought to be leaders in society. He had
nothing but contempt for the " 'new white man' representing

the masses—self-reliant, forceful but unmellowed by long re-sponsibility." If men with long experience in responsibility could not be in positions of leadership, Murphy wanted to educate these new white men as quickly as possible to provide them with at least the appearance of "culture."[24]

Murphy used the word "culture" with great frequency. Its meaning was not precisely clear, but seemed to involve not only education and wealth, but also a certain gentility which came from the past, and from many generations of genteel and educated people. Men with "culture" had an in-bred ability to comprehend a situation. They were not moved by the passions of the moment and could guide the passions of others. A democracy, Murphy felt, must see to it that culture could flourish freely. Culture had an obliga-tion to sustain itself, for "though majorities may often be wrong, so long as culture exists there will be someone to oppose oppression."[25]

The most carefully thought out expression of these ideas of elite leadership was in Murphy's article "The Task of the Leader."[26] Here he started with the assumption that just men, men of "finer, stronger fibre and of a responsive public conscience," were rare among humanity. These men provided the "mind" of society and must be treasured. Murphy joined Edmund Burke in condemning the French Revolution not so much for its violence (though he condemned that) as for its slaying of the "mind" of French society. Likewise, the tra-gedy of the Civil War was that "In those graves that marked the march of her armies the *mind* of the South was buried." The men of this type left in the South had upon them the "burden of intelligence and character." This type of per-son was "bound by the responsibilities of leadership."

The task of this natural elite was to act as a balance wheel, a gyroscope against the wild careenings of a too democratic society. The natural leader "has never learned to weigh influence in the crude scale of numbers." He is in com-munication not with those people who happen to surround him at any one moment, but with thousands of his kind, with the traditions of leadership, to which he must be true. When the whole world had been turned upside down, the first quality of leadership was not aggressiveness, but self-containment or moral steadiness.

Thus, while Murphy marched in step with the Progressive army, his goal was not a welfare state, the victory of the masses over their oppressors, nor a centralized, efficient society. In condemning child labor, and working for better schools and better race relations, Murphy was trying to preserve or recreate a stable world in the face of threatening chaos.

6

REFORM AND THE DEMOS

Robert M. La Follette

Robert M. La Follette enthusiastically embraced the tumult of American politics which Edgar Gardner Murphy found so offensive, a difference in taste indicative of fundamentally divergent philosophies. While both men wanted to protect the victims of industrialization, Murphy attempted the task by limiting democracy, La Follette by extending it. The changes he proposed resembled those of Jane Addams in their attempt not so much to create an orderly society in the face of impending chaos as to take risks in a quest for social justice.

In the classic tradition of American politics, La Follette was born in a log cabin, and very nearly became President of the United States.[1] Over several generations, Robert's ancestors had moved westward a state or two at a time: Virginia, Kentucky, Indiana, and finally Wisconsin, where he was born. Young Bob never knew his father, who died when the boy was only eight months old. His mother taught him to revere his father's memory, and when she remarried the boy kept the name La Follette instead of taking that of his stepfather, John Saxton. A prominent and prosperous citizen of the town of Argyle, Saxton had a reputation for being a stern disciplinarian and hard taskmaster as well as something of a skinflint. He was a vigorous Baptist, fond of preaching eternal damnation, especially to young boys. Bob

La Follette may have respected his stepfather, but he never developed anything like affection for him.

This lack of warmth between the two, together with La Follette's driving sense of ambition, soon prompted the boy to strike out on his own. At about the time that John Saxton's declining business affairs forced the family to move back to the La Follette farm, Bob took a job as a barber at the Argyle hotel in an effort to support himself away from home while he attended high school. Although his stepfather's age and failing strength soon obliged the four-teen-year-old lad to leave school to manage the family farm, he never abandoned his goal of getting an education.

In 1872, when La Follette was eighteen years old, his step-father died. Bob worked the farm for another year, then renting it to his brother-in-law, he took his mother and younger sister to Madison where he intended to complete his education. Unprepared for college, he spent some months in preparatory schools until he could enter the University of Wisconsin, then an institution of some four hundred students. To earn his way he taught school, sold books, and did whatever odd jobs he could find. After his freshman year, he borrowed four hundred dollars, bought the university newspaper, and earned a meager living as editor and publisher. He took part in university dramatics, politics, and oratorical contests, and studied as little as he could get away with. In an elementary German class he met a bright and thoroughly sensible young lady named Belle Case. The two were attracted to each other almost immediately and were married directly after they graduated.

In later years, La Follette emphasized the strong influence which President John Bascom of the University had had on him, yet the exact nature of this influence is hard to describe. Bascom was something of a universal scholar, who wrote on religion, economics, sociology, aesthetics, ethics, literature, psychology, and philosophy. He was a deeply re-ligious man, but not at all other-worldly, believing firmly in progress on this earth through human effort.[2] Robert La

Follette was neither pious nor scholarly, yet he said that no one influenced him more than this pious scholar. Apparently La Follette thought of himself as carrying into political life Bascom's intense integrity and moral purposefulness.

Upon graduation La Follette could not decide whether to enter the theater, law, or the academic life. After consulting Belle, he chose the law and passed his bar examination after only seven months of study. By this time, at the age of twenty-six, he had already displayed the qualities which were to characterize his career—a flair for drama and public performance, an ability to move people with his words, and a fierce determination to arrive at his objective.

Determination was especially noticeable in his first attempt at political office, the county attorneyship, which he sought immediately after passing his bar exam. He could not persuade the regular Republican organization to back him, so he ran and won without party support. He made a good reputation in spite of meager experience, and in 1884, still over the opposition of party regulars, waged a successful fight for national office. As a Representative, he served in the Congress which passed the Interstate Commerce Act, the Sherman Anti-Trust Act, and the McKinley tariff. He worked hard and quickly earned a reputation for intelligence and competence. After two more successful campaigns for Congress, he was beaten in the Democratic landslide of 1890. It was when he was out of office during the 'nineties that La Follette's political course was determined.

His role in state politics during these years is somewhat unclear. He pictured himself as a young knight fighting bossism in Wisconsin, but the most careful analyst of Wisconsin politics says that La Follette opposed the "bosses" largely because they would not let him join them.[3] Whatever the case, by 1894 he and a group of friends were openly fighting the regular Republicans of the state. In 1894 the insurgents backed Nils P. Haugen, a long-time friend of La Follette, in an unsuccessful campaign for the governorship, and in 1896 and again in 1898, La Follette failed in his effort to win the office for himself. After the second defeat, he gave up the frontal attack on the stone wall of the regular organization. Instead, he tried to go around it. With less furor than usual, but with better preparation, he found financial backing and built up an organization on foundations other than friendship. Since most of the regular Republican leaders were aging, and since there was no obvious line of succession, La Follette saw his chance. Cautiously and quietly, he smoothed over old antagonisms without creating new ones, and in 1900 he was nominated by a united party which fought and won the gubernatorial election in what was known as the "harmony campaign."

With La Follette's first message to the legislature, the harmony came to an end. He asked for those measures for which he had vigorously campaigned during the last six years: *ad valorem* taxation of railroads in place of the existing license fee system, and a direct primary law. The stalwart Republicans who had helped elect him then deserted and stifled his program in the legislature. Determined that the same thing should not be repeated in the 1903 session, La Follette fought hard for a sympathetic Assembly and Senate. He treated the election as a simple choice between good and evil by telling his constituents that they could vote for him, democracy and honesty, or for the stalwarts, bossism and economic exploitation. His powerful gift of oratory, his ability to make complex issues seem simple, and his carefully prepared campaign, triumphed over the combined opposition of Democrats and conservative Republicans. He carried a majority of the lower house into office with him, but he failed to win control of the Senate. His primary law and *ad valorem* taxation bills passed, but not in the form he wanted. The final test was to come in the 1904 election.

In the pre-convention campaign, La Follette's forces abandoned hope of a united stand with the stalwarts. In fact, the stalwarts eventually bolted the convention. This proved to be their undoing, for with La Follette's victory, the stalwart organization fell apart, and although La Follette received a plurality rather than a majority of the popular vote, he secured control of both the executive and legislative branches of government. La Follette quickly forced his program through the House and Senate. The legislature established a railroad commission; made primary elections a reality; created a civil service commission; strengthed an already existing tax commission; and adopted anti-lobbying, banking, and conservation legislation. The upper house also elected him to the United States Senate. La Follette had denied any plans to seek the senatorship, but with the success of his program assured in Wisconsin, he welcomed the return to national politics.

In the United States Senate, La Follette started very much in a minority position. By persevering, by standing firm, and by holding to his ideals, he became the leader of a band of Republican rebels who eventually held the balance of power in the Senate. Within a few years of returning to national politics, he became the undisputed leader of the progressive Republicans in Washington and very nearly their principal spokesman in the nation.

From the very beginning of Robert M. La Follette's political career, he was an independent-minded, headstrong, young man. He ran for country attorney against the wishes of the regular Republican organization, and what was worse, he won. From then on, although he stayed within the Republican party, sometime just barely within it, he saw himself as a brave fighter for the sake of truth. This was by no means all pose, for he was frequently in opposition to much of his party. But La Follette also knew that his reputation as an embattled underdog was a potent weapon to use against his opponents, and he exploited it even in those circumstances were he sided with the majority. Although his role as a martyr for the common man brought La Follette great success, he experienced difficulty in sustaining what was essentially a paradoxical position—being both a martyr and a success. Perhaps it was this which obliged him to be constantly on the watch for issues in which he could side with the underdog;

perhaps it was this which obliged him to be constantly in search of bigger, more powerful enemies against whom to do battle. Thus be began by attacking the regular Republicans in Wisconsin, then went on to tackle the stand-pat elements in the United States Senate, all of corporate greed in America, the perfidious Theodore Roosevelt, and, during the war years, the nation itself.[4]

In view of La Follette's assertion that the "interests" were against him but that the people were for him, it is sometimes difficult to tell whether his expressions of confidence in the popular will were declarations of heartfelt faith, or mere political maneuvering. Perhaps his paeans to the rural life were at least partly tactical. He spoke of Wisconsin's population as being made up of the best elements from Europe—the farmers—who had the time for contemplation that the city dwellers lacked. He wanted Wisconsin to encourage immigration, but to the farms, not to the cities.

Although his praise for the wisdom of farmers may have been simply an attempt to flatter voters, La Follette had a deep confidence in the ability of an informed electorate to decide who should represent them and what the broad direction of policy should be. He assumed that popular government would be sound government, and he never seemed to consider the possibility of a misguided popular movement. There was a "mysterious power in an enlightened democracy which finally marshalls public opinion for the right and makes it irresistible." This mysterious power was nothing else than simple rationality, which all men possessed. La Follette approved of a Colorado law which would have provided modest public financing of political campaigns. All the politicians had to do was get information to the voters, who could then rationally choose the best man or best program. "The American people have again and again proven themselves capable of good governing," he insisted, "no corrupt political ring has ever entrenched itself so strongly in power that its misgovernment could not be terminated when the people were once aroused.'"⁶ In asking the Wisconsin Senate to pass a direct primary law, he said:

> It is of the essence of republican government that the citizen should act for himself directly wherever possible. In the exercise of no other right is this so important as the nomination of candidates for office. It is of primary importance that the public official should hold himself directly accountable to the citizens.⁷

That popular government is both necessary and sufficient to insure good government was an argument he repeated from his earliest horse-and-buggy campaigns to the end of his life.⁸

La Follette was not very precise about the structure of the society which these paragons of rationality inhabited. He was aware of the existence of economic classes, but seemed to see only two classes and these only vaguely: the extorters or "the interests" on the one hand and the victims or "the people" on the other. This is similar to Gompers' simple dichotomy between the workers and the capitalists, but La Follette was less exclusive in his allies than Gompers was. Workers, farmers, professional men, white-collar workers, all were "the people." The enemy was confined to a small group of financiers and corporation directors whom La Follette usually thought of as Easterners.⁹

To a degree which was surprising in a man whose main concern was with economic issues, La Follette seemed more clearly aware of racial than of economic cleavages in society. La Follette's awareness of racial differences was not racism, for he was not hostile to any race. He argued that racial conflict came not from the fact that one race was inferior to another, but from the fact that no race had the necessary wisdom and moral strength to stem prejudice. Thus he could praise one book for showing the artistic gifts of American Indians, and another for sympathetically describing the growth of modern China.¹⁰

Nevertheless, he wanted to exclude Asiatics from the United States because a society in which different races lived together could not avoid conflict. "Neither we nor the Asiatics are sufficiently advanced in civilization to mingle in the fellowship that makes for peace." La Follette cited conflict between various races in the Near and Middle East and between whites and blacks in the United States to show the dangers of a multi-racial community.[11]

His views on education as a determinant of ability were ambiguous. He thought of himself as a stump educator and he respected no man more than John Bascom of the University of Wisconsin. He urged the importance of education in rural areas. In arguing for women's suffrage, one of his reasons was that women were frequently better educated than their husbands. Moreover, he placed great reliance on commissions of trained experts. Yet he insisted that every adult, regardless of education, had the wisdom to determine governmental policies, and he would not agree that men of education, or any other group, knew best what policies the state or nation should follow.[12]

If men were rational, whence came the evils La Follette was trying to eliminate? Like Jane Addams, he blamed the industrial system which created cities, the breeding ground of crime and corruption. Cities, products of commercial greed rather than human needs, created an environment which, when combined with atomization of work, inevitably brutalized and dehumanized the individual. Though different in character, dehumanization was as much a product of industrialism as a bridge or a locomotive were. Moreover, it led to a variety of social ills. To La Follette, crime and poverty were products of environment, not individual defects. As social problems they could be cured by social remedies.[13] Yet, once having blamed the system, La Follette seems to have had no clear idea as to the mechanisms which led to crime and poverty. His attitude was not so much a philosophic position as a meagerly thought out hunch.

Whatever the mechanism, big business was the villain, a conspiracy which prospered through the cannabalism of corporate merger to create the social ills of the nation. "The

general opinion west of the Hudson," he said, "is that the
home of frenzied finance is dealing a shell game against the
nation in which the nation has not even a gambling chance
of winning." The high cost of living was due to an artifi-
cially high price level which he attributed to the tariff and
monopolistic manipulation. High taxes were due to special
privileges granted to grain speculators, fertilizer trusts, meat
packers, and above all to railroads.[14]

The railroads were La Follette's *bête noir*. He won his
governorship and senatorship largely on the basis of his anti-
railroad position, and his early campaign speeches concentrated so heavily on railroad abuses that one might think
that La Follette considered them the only evil worth talking
about. However, although until 1905 he made the railroad question the chief political issue in Wisconsin, and although he devoted over two-thirds of his first two legislative
messages to railroad regulation and taxation, once he had
achieved his goals he went on to advocate a wide variety of
other reforms.[15]

Corruption of the nation's economic life was not the chief
crime that La Follette attributed to corporate rapacity. On
the contrary, he worried much more about the corruption
of the nation's political life. From the very beginning, he
sounded the theme that the great trusts threatened democratic institutions. Partly political tactics, partly another stick
with which to beat his enemies, his views stemmed from a
genuine fear of the threat to democracy posed by big business. Although La Follette could have appealed to the voters
on purely economic grounds, throughout the period from the
days when he was a twice-defeated candidate for governor to
his days in the United States Senate he chose instead to press
the political argument upon his constituents.[16]

Corporate influence on politics worked in a variety of
ways. To prevent lobbying abuses, La Follette proposed a bill
to limit the right of persuasion to duly constituted committee
hearings. He also favored a law forbidding the issuance of

railroad passes, and he tried to expose officials who were unduly influenced by big business. As a counterpoise to the controlled press, he started his own magazine in 1909.[17]

In spite of the power wielded by the "interests," La Follette remained optimistic. He willingly suffered repeated reverses, confident that eventually his reform proposals and his own candidacy would succeed. Progress, he felt, could not be stopped, for the Progressive movement was part of a natural continuum of reform ideas which extended from the Revolution in an unbroken line through the Civil War, Grange, and Populist party to contemporary America. The cause of justice, he argued, was "not a mere wave of sentiment that ebbs and flows . . . but principle. Principle does not recede."[18]

Yet progress could not be achieved without leaders to educate the electorate, to point out problems, and to suggest solutions. He saw himself in this role and respected Theodore Roosevelt for being such an effective leader. Although there were many "jolts and jars which made our bones ache" when Roosevelt was President, the nation was at least kept awake."

> The White House is not merely an office where affairs are administered. It is a rostrum from which lectures are spoken; a pulpit from which sermons are preached; a source from which must inevitably flow either stimulus or sedative.

The task of the leader was to stimulate and educate citizens to their responsibilities.[19]

Once the electorate had fulfilled these responsibilities by determining the broad outlines of policy, La Follette thought details of procedure best left to scientific experts. He believed firmly that there could be experts in all fields, that society could and should be steered by specialists toward its chosen goals. He based his support of the city manager system on his confidence in experts; he wanted a permanent, professionally staffed tariff commission; he favored establishing a professorship of criminology at the University of Wisconsin; he frequently used university experts; and he supported the new concept of scientific management. All legislation, he said, should be based on scientific study.[20]

With goals established by expressions of the popular will and means worked out by experts, La Follette saw no value in the restraining influence of tradition. The Constitution and the Declaration of Independence, although the basis for American government, were neither sufficient nor inviolable. The Senate was originally established as an aristocratic check on democracy, but it ought not to be maintained as such. The fact that the Founding Fathers had not thought of the direct primary did not preclude the necessity for one.[21]

La Follette thought that these changes should not be made timidly. The nation should go forward a step at a time, but each should be a full step.[22] In a sense this reflected a stubbornness which would not compromise with political necessities. However, La Follette's experience in Wisconsin was that success could be won by hammering away, year after year, at unchanging, uncompromising goals. His inflexibility seemed to please his constituents. Is it any wonder that he, like Samuel Gompers, stuck to a method which had proved so successful?

It was this philosophy which brought him into repeated conflict with Theodore Roosevelt. President Roosevelt, with many more pressures on him than any senator, often was willing to accept legislation which La Follette considered to be only half a step. "The Pres[ident] has a passion for getting as many things started as possible," La Follette wrote to his wife. "A good bill can be passed now; but the passage of a makeshift will defer good legislation for ten years." In his autobiography, which was at least partly an apologia aimed at Roosevelt, La Follette wrote "in legislation *no bread* is often better than *half a loaf*. I believe it is better to be beaten and come right back at the next session and make a fight for a thorough-going law." On the occasion of one bill, La Follette wrote the President, "the interests of the public will be better served by temporary defeat of an effective measure . . . than by compromise on a bill which sounds well in the title but is weak or silent on vital points." He spoke critically of the Interstate Commerce and the Sherman Anti-Trust acts because they did not go far enough. He opposed the Hepburn Act because he thought it did not adequately strengthen the Interstate Commerce Commission. He opposed the Mann-Elkins Act for similar reasons.[23]

This inflexibility appeared, even to some of his allies, as unjustified mulishness and a refusal to recognize political necessities. It is true that he often disagreed with the master politician, Theodore Roosevelt, but he too was a shrewd and experienced strategist and it need not be La Follette who was always wrong. Moreover, the Wisconsin senator could sometimes bend with the political wind—at least a little—as in his harmony campaign in 1900, and in 1907, in his acceptance of distasteful amendments to one of his bills in order to get it passed.[24]

Although La Follette came from an agrarian society, his program was not aimed at preserving a rural idyll, but at creating a good society in a world whose urban and industrial nature he fully understood. He was in close touch with Jane Addams, approving of her work, which like his recognized that cities could not be dismantled and a rural freeholding society re-established. With Miss Addams, he recognized a large degree of governmental responsibility for public welfare. As governor he urged the introduction of safety laws for railroads, a minimum wage law, and abrogation of the legal doctrine of contributory negligence which released employers from nearly all responsibility for industrial accidents. After he went to the Senate, the La Follette organization in Wisconsin passed a workman's compensation act and created an industrial commission to supervise and enforce the nation's most comprehensive child labor, hours, and safety legislation. In the Senate his opposition to the Hepburn Act was based on the broadest grounds of governmental responsibility for the general welfare.[25]

By 1909, La Follette was willing to go very far indeed

toward a welfare state. He insisted that poverty was not due to inability but to exploitation and he saw a new day coming when "society would be formed in which common responsibility for the general welfare was recognized." He endorsed Sidney Webb's proposal of a "National Minimum," a standard of living set by the government below which no one would be allowed to sink. The minimum should include not only food and shelter, but also recreation, sanitation, education, and the opportunity for the enjoyment of art. He vigorously applauded David Lloyd-George's budget of 1909, which was widely regarded, especially by its opponents, as the entering wedge for socialism in England. La Follette consistently supported the formation of unions and their exercise of economic power. He favored a federal income tax which would and should inquire into what was heretofore the private affairs of citizens. He praised the new sociological jurisprudence, especially the judge who said, "What we know as men we cannot profess to be ignorant of as judges." By 1912, La Follette could go so far as to insist that the usefulness of individualism was over and that more co-operation was necessary.[26]

Likewise, La Follette recognized that big business was a necessary part of the new society and could not be destroyed. He did not oppose bigness but rather the dominance of an entire industry by one or two giant corporations. Therefore he proposed legislation making 40 per cent control of any industry by one corporation as *prima facie* evidence of the type of unreasonable restraint of trade prohibited by the Sherman Act.[27] Although the practical difficulties in administering this amendment would have been great, the proposal was not designed to create a shopkeeper economy and might well have preserved competition while permitting economic growth.

La Follette may have been too convinced of his own righteousness, may have been too stubborn, but he saw clearly the outline of the new industrial American and he proposed reforms appropriate to the new age. With Theodore Roosevelt, Jane Addams, and Sidney Webb, he was convinced that government at all levels had responsibilities toward its citizens, and he urged that these responsibilities be met by vigorous action. La Follette marched in the army of reform not toward the society envisioned by Samuel Gompers or Edgar Gardner Murphy, but toward a society much like that envisioned by Franklin D. Roosevelt.

Conclusion

American reform thought encompassed tremendous variety, a variety, moreover, confined neither to superficial problems nor to questions of procedure. The disagreement among reformers was over basic questions about the nature of man and of society, those questions, in other words, about which all Americans supposedly either hold like views or hold no views at all.

For instance, of the reformers whose social assumptions have been analyzed, only two, Jane Addams and Robert M. La Follette, were unqualified in their endorsement of the essential nature of man. These two, one functioning in a rural state, the other in the nation's second largest city, were firmly convinced of the essential goodness of human nature. These two alone were confident that man's social salvation could be reached simply by freeing him from the chains of a misconstructed society. The other four had misgivings of varying degrees about human goodness. Senator Beveridge thought that much restraint was necessary to counteract disorderly or destructive human impulses. For Samuel Gompers, humans were a selfish lot. While their selfishness was not a quality he condemned, his view was certainly far less benign than that of either La Follette or Miss Addams. The members of the Civic Federation shared with Edgar Gardner Murphy a distrust for the masses. The Northern businessmen and the Southern minister were both of the opinion that the control of society should be in the hands of the best people. By "best" they meant men of property and gentility, although the businessmen might have put less emphasis on the latter.

For some of the reformers, the natural goodness of man

meant a natural rationality. Certainly, the faith in human rationality was strongest in La Follette, who thought that national policy could be determined merely by stating issues in great detail, then ascertaining the popular will. Beveridge gave men considerable powers of reason in that narrow area where destiny gave them choice. Murphy and the Civic Federation thought that some people could be rational, but that rationality was a product of training and breeding, not a quality inherent in all mankind. Gompers had faith in the ability of men to reason their way through to valid conclusions, but he preferred to rely on trial by combat for determining the direction and speed of social change. Jane Addams, while she had great faith in human ability, would not have called this ability rationality. For Jane Addams, each person had an instinctive, non-verbal, non-rational, poetic empathy with reality which enabled him intuitively to arrive at proper results.

How did these reformers see man in the aggregate? Their views ranged over the entire spectrum of attitudes on the structure of society. At one end was Jane Addams, who saw society as a single entity in which individuals were joined by their common humanity. At the other end of the scale was Edgar Gardner Murphy, who saw society fragmented into dozens of pieces. Close to Jane Addams in this spectrum was Albert Beveridge, who also saw a great deal of unity. There were a few, broad, racial streams with little in common, but within each stream individuals were closely united. Here his emphasis differed from that of Miss Addams, for he considered each person merely a special case of the general aggregate, and therefore of small importance. Jane Addams never considered any individual *merely* a special case. Since each person partook of the common humanity, each was, for her, infinitely valuable. Gompers thought that society had divisions, but unlike Murphy, he saw only two. In this opinion, he was joined by the Civic Federation which also saw strata in society, but the Chicago elite looked down from the upper stratum, while Gompers looked up from the lower one. La Follette's views on the question of social divisions was somewhat unclear. He seemed to think the great mass of society comprised a single group, without important divisions, upon whom a few selfish men were trying to prey.

Samuel Gompers thought that the divisions between classes should be emphasized. For all the other reformers, by contrast, social differences were an evil to be minimized or eliminated. Jane Addams believed that the elimination of these differences was the greatest good toward which she could work. Edgar Gardner Murphy also aimed at eliminating divisions among men, but he was less hopeful about achieving the goal. For the Civic Federation, La Follette, and Beveridge, class differences were of lesser import, but probably none thought they could be eliminated.

What was the relationship between an individual and the groups of which he was a member? Were individuals being submerged by groups? Was this good or bad? Jane Addams, Albert Beveridge, and Samuel Gompers all saw an increase in some sort of consciousness of group. For Miss Addams this meant a consciousness of one's duties toward all of society; for Beveridge it meant a consciousness of one's identity within a race; for Gompers it meant an increase in class consciousness. Thus all three welcomed the development of some form of group relationship, but Jane Addams disapproved of just that type of class consciousness which Gompers wanted. For Robert La Follette and the Civic Federation, the question was not important, but Edgar Gardner Murphy did see a certain amount of group consciousness in society. He welcomed it, as long as it was based on race and not on class, but he was careful to distinguish between racial consciousness, which he applauded, and racial chauvinism, which he deplored.

The reaction to an increased emphasis on groups rather than individuals is closely related to a basic dilemma in social philosophy. This involves two of the items in the trinity of the French Revolution. *Liberté* and *egalité* were closely linked in the eighteenth century. Since then, the concepts that these words represent have often become contradictory. *Liberté* has been used as a slogan to support the right to be unequal, especially in the matter of acquiring wealth, while *egalité* has been used to support the right to minimum standards of social and economic welfare, the realization of which have often been predicated upon a system of graduated taxation designed to prevent individuals rising to great wealth or sinking to abject poverty. Of the reformers treated here, Jane Addams voted strongest for *egalité*, with La Follette close behind. Both were less interested in allowing scope for advancement than in protecting those who had not advanced from those who had. Both would have denied that liberty was thereby decreased, for they saw the restraints imposed by poverty as greater threats to liberty than any conceivable welfare measures.

Senator Beveridge might appear an ally of Miss Addams and La Follette, but his rejection of a laissez-faire interpretation of *liberté* sprang not so much from a love of *egalité* as from his belief that centralized power was necessary to prevent social waste and disorder. He was willing to limit liberty in order to prevent these evils. Samuel Gompers, though he might have said that his goal was simply *egalité*, staunchly defended the *liberté* side of the dilemma because he wanted the working class to be free to get as much of the national wealth as it could. Both Edgar Gardner Murphy and the Civic Federation scorned the idea of equality. They knew that people were not equal and believed firmly that the most able should be free to rise to positions of wealth, responsibility, and power.

Albert Beveridge respected power as the force which kept society together and moved it in the right direction. He thought that to be most efficient, power should be centralized. Jane Addams agreed with him on the need for centralization, but not because she respected power. Rather, she assumed that since society was unified, or at least should be, a centralization of power was natural. La Follette shared this willingness to centralize power. He felt that certain objectives could not be accomplished in any other way. Gompers was willing to see power concentrated, but not by government. Perhaps, it would be more accurate to say that he wanted to see power polarized between a unified capitalist class on the one hand and a unified working class on the other. Again on this question, Edgar Gardner Murphy and the Civic Federation agreed in their opposition to any high degree of centralization.

All these attitudes toward power were expressed most frequently as attitudes about government. For the Civic Federation and Samuel Gompers, government was simply one of many institutions in society and both regarded it as something of a nuisance at best. Edgar Gardner Murphy also seemed to think of government as simply one among many institutions, but he gave it a somewhat larger and more benign place. For La Follette, as for Miss Addams, government was the prime instrument of social progress. However, for Jane Addams, as well as for Albert J. Beveridge, government was far more than a tool for accomplishing certain ends. It was a transcendent expression or incarnation of society's existence.

All of these people were reformers, so all had to believe in the possibility of some progress. They did not agree on how much was possible. Here again, Jane Addams and La Follette joined in recognizing great possibilities for improvement. Beveridge gave an ambivalent response because he seemed unable to make up his mind on the question of how much was wrong with society. Gompers saw a laboriously slow movement in the right direction; the Civic Federation saw the possibility of change, but not much necessity; Murphy recognized the necessity, but was not very confident of results.

Jane Addams and La Follette agreed that human beings could control the speed and direction of social change. Both believed that if enough people wanted certain social goals, the goals could and should be attained. Joining with them on this issue was the Civic Federation. Gompers, too, had confidence in human ability to control human destiny. As a practical man, he knew that every step of the way would require struggle, that temporary retreats were bound to occur, but he had little doubt that over the long haul men could slowly create the kind of society they wanted. Edgar Gardner Murphy had considerable doubts. Some changes in society were within human capacity—but just as certainly there were other areas where human beings could not control their destiny. Beveridge saw men as puny creatures, controlled rather than controlling.

Only two of the reformers thought it necessary to make any explicit statement about how men acquired knowledge of society. These two, Jane Addams and Robert La Follette, were also the ones with the greatest confidence in the ability of humans to control social change. Both emphasized the need for systematic study of any social question before trying to act. In part, this was a measure of the responsibility of these two reformers. If our fate is in our hands, they seemed to say, we must make sure we know what we are doing before we act. La Follette, therefore, always buttressed his position on railroad and tariff legislation with facts and figures, and Jane Addams, though more publicist than academician, nevertheless strongly encouraged the new science of sociology.

The reformers also held widely divergent views on historical causation. Jane Addams supported sociological study because she believed that men were products of their environment, that the course of human history was determined by sociological law. Beveridge shared this belief in determinism, but he thought that the underlying force was inexorable destiny. Samuel Gompers, by contrast, was as complete an economic determinist as could be found. He may have rejected all types of socialism, but he did not reject the socialist belief that economic forces shape society. Edgar Gardner Murphy, although he did not stress theology in his reform writings, must have believed that society was ultimately controlled by divine will. What the Civic Federation thought about historical determinism is not clear.

La Follette put heavy emphasis on economic forces shaping society, but he also had considerable sympathy for Jane Addams' more general environmentalism.

The agent of change for La Follette, Jane Addams, and Beveridge was clearly a central governmental authority. These three had no fear of extending government, and it was obvious to them that no agency except government could do the job. For Gompers the agent of change was the automatic functioning of class conflict. Both Edgar Gardner Murphy and the Civic Federation put their emphasis on the foresight, wisdom, and ability of an elite.

What was all this change for? What were the goals of these reformers? What were their visions of the good life? Here is where historians who claim Americans do not have an ideology may be on firm ground. Most of the Americans examined here did not have a very clear picture of the society they would have considered ideal. Jane Addams probably had the clearest set of goals: a welfare state responsible for the material, intellectual, and spiritual well-being of every individual. La Follette joined her in this vision, but his crystal ball was somewhat more clouded. By 1912, Beveridge also cheered the hosts of the welfare state, but more for the state than the welfare. Edgar Gardner Murphy saw a trail of endless struggle in the pursuit of justice. The goal was Christian brotherhood, but he added few details. Gompers refused explicitly to envision a set of goals and the Civic Federation had not the vision to try.

There is no evidence that these reformers were motivated by a concern that their social, economic, and political status relative to men of great wealth was declining. Jane Addams, a woman of middling means, did not fear that the rich would usurp her position. On the contrary, she felt guilt at having so much wealth herself, and wished for a status revolution in which the poor would be raised. Gompers gloried in being on a low status level by clinging to his identification with the working class. Did Beveridge and La Follette feel that their position as lawyers in cities of moderate size was being threatened? Perhaps somewhere deep within themselves they did, but if so there is no evidence of it. Both Edgar Gardner Murphy and the Civic Federation were worried far more about being overrun from below than overshadowed from above.

Not only did reform thought exhibit variety, it was a variety which can not be organized by any simple schema. The bipolar system of categories customarily used by American historians does not fit at all. The Progressives were neither all "Jeffersonian" nor all "Hamiltonian." On the contrary, most of them combined elements of both philosophies. Edgar Gardner Murphy, for example, the most explicit proponent of the Hamiltonian belief in rule by an elite also wanted the Jeffersonian system of decentralized government. Robert La Follette, the most thorough-going believer in the capacity of Jefferson's common man for self-government, also envisioned the creation of a welfare state modelled along the lines of Hamilton's centralized national authority. And although Samuel Gompers welcomed industrialization (Hamiltonian), he strongly advocated laissez-faire (a no less thoroughly un-Hamiltonian view).

Herbert Croly's dictum that the Progressives used Hamiltonian means for Jeffersonian ends also does not seem very helpful. Which were ends and which were means? Did Albert Beveridge want a powerful centralized government to recreate a democratic rural society, or was a powerful government an end in itself? Jane Addams wanted to use government to create a co-operative commonwealth, not a community of yeoman farmers. The Civic Federation wanted a decentralized government to permit elite rule: Jeffersonian means for Hamiltonian ends. In fact, terms like "Jeffersonian" and "Hamiltonian" are usually catch phrases used to evoke emotional responses, not tools of analysis or even useful shorthand. Indeed, more may be learned about America by analyzing the misuse of the terms than by actually trying to apply them.

In the face of Gompers' insistence on laissez-faire and La Follette's on the welfare state, a division between rural and urban reformers seems even less useful as a scheme of synthesis. The division between forward-looking and backward-looking reformers holds out still less promise. In the complexities of social philosophies of various reformers, can anyone decide which proposals looked forward and which backward?

Legend relates that J. P. Morgan was once asked what would happen to the stock market. With clear vision he answered, "It will fluctuate." In the same way, the best answer to the question, what did American reformers think about the nature of man and of society is: "They disagreed."

In short, the American intellectual landscape is neither desert nor monotonous plain. It has hills, valleys, hidden caves, deserts, and seas. It is worth exploring.

Notes

PREFACE

[1] Indications of the revived interest in closing the gap between Populism and Progressivism can be found in Norman Pollack, *The Populist Response to Industrial America* (Cambridge, Massachusetts, 1962), and in Francis P. Weisenburger's review of John Higham's *Reconstruction of American History* (Harper Torchbook, 1961) in the *Mississippi Valley Historical Review*, 49:362-363 (September, 1962). The first group is best represented by Richard Hofstadter's *Age of Reform* (New York, 1955), George E. Mowry's *The California Progressives* (Berkeley, 1952), and Daniel Aaron's, *Men of Good Hope: A Study of American Progressives* (New York, 1951). Aaron approves of the limited goals, while Hofstadter does not. The second group is best represented in Roy Lubove, "The Twentieth Century City: The Progressive as Municipal Reformer," in *Mid-America*, 41:195-209 (October, 1959), and Andrew M. Scott, "The Progressive Era in Perspective," in the *Journal of Politics*, 21:685-701 (November, 1951). The third group includes Arthur S. Link, *Woodrow Wilson, The Road to the White House* (Princeton, 1947); George E. Mowry, *The Era of Theodore Roosevelt* (New York, 1958); Paul Glad, *The Trumpet Soundeth* (Lincoln, 1960), and Eric Goldman, *Rendezvous with Destiny* (New York, 1952). Mowry tends toward the first group, Goldman toward the second.

CHAPTER 1: JANE ADDAMS

[1] The biographical portion of this chapter is based on James Weber Linn, *Jane Addams* (New York, 1935), Jane Addams, *Twenty Years at Hull House* (New York, 1910), and Robert H. Bremner, *From the Depths* (New York, 1956).

[2] Addams, *Newer Ideals of Peace* (New York, 1907), 70; *The Spirit of Youth in the City Streets* (New York, 1909), 3-9.

[3] Addams, "Public Recreation and Social Morality," in *Charities*, 18:494 (August, 1907); "Reaction of Modern Life upon Religious Education," in *Religious Education*, 4:24 (April, 1909); "Reaction of Moral Instruction on Social Reform," in *Survey*, 22:17 (August, 1909); *The Spirit of Youth*, 18, 139-162.

[4] *Ibid.*, 52.

[5]Addams, *A New Conscience and an Ancient Evil* (New York, 1912), 123–124; *The Spirit of Youth,* 118. See also, *ibid.,* 107.

[6]*Ibid.,* 10; Addams, "Public Recreation and Social Morality," 492–493, 494; "Child Labor and Pauperism," in *Charities,* 11:303 (October, 1903); "Problems of Municipal Administration," in the *American Journal of Sociology,* 10:428 (January, 1905); Addams *et. al., Philanthropy and Social Progress* (New York, 1893), 34–35.

[7]Addams, "Problems of Municipal Administration," 432; "Public Recreation and Social Morality," 494; and interview with Lea Taylor, June 11, 1963.

[8]Addams, "Charity and Social Justice," in the *North American Review,* 192:78 (July, 1910); "Present Crisis in Trades-Union Morals," in *ibid.,* 179: 192–193 (August, 1904); *The Spirit of Youth,* 107; *Newer Ideals of Peace,* 64–65.

[9]Addams, "Subtle Problems of Charity," in *Atlantic,* 83:163–164, 166 (February, 1899); *The Spirit of Youth,* 9.

[10]Addams, "Problems of Municipal Administration," 432; "A Challenge to the Contemporary Church," in *Survey,* 28:196, 198 (May 4, 1912).

[11]Addams, *A New Conscience,* 167, 100, 110; *The Spirit of Youth,* 26–27, 30–44. It is perhaps significant for Jane Addams' own feelings that she always assumed that young girls went wrong through the perfidy of evil men. The rewards expected by these men she termed "hideous."

[12]Addams, "Crisis in Trades-Union Morals," 180–181; "Trades Unions and Public Duty," in the *American Journal of Sociology,* 4:461 (January, 1899); to Mary Addams Linn, April 1, 1889, in the Addams Correspondence; *A New Conscience,* 161.

[13]*Ibid.,* 33; Addams, "A New Impulse to an Old Gospel," in *Forum,* 14:350–351 (November, 1892); "Subtle Problems of Charity," 163.

[14]Addams, *Democracy and Social Ethics* (New York, 1902), 256; "A Modern Lear—The Strike at Pullman," in *Survey,* 29:135 (November, 1912). This article almost shows a clear understanding of the shortcomings of George Pullman's paternalism, yet in casting Mr. Pullman as Lear and the workers as Cordelia, Miss Addams herself betrays a condescension. Was George Pullman simply a well-meaning but short-sighted father? Were the workers children, who, whatever their legitimate grievances, failed to appreciate the benefits they received?

[15]Addams to Mary Rozet Smith, 1893, in the Addams Correspondence in the Swarthmore College Peace Collection.

[16]Addams, "Charity and Social Justice," 68–81; *Newer Ideals of Peace,* 15, 94; "Problems of Municipal Administration," 438.

[17]Edith Abbott, "Hull House of Jane Addams," in the *Social Service Review,* 26:334–338 (September, 1952); "Grace Abbott and Hull House," in *ibid.,* 24:374–394, 493–518 (September and December, 1950).

[18]Addams, "Subtle Problems of Charity," 177; *Democracy and Social Ethics,* 299, where she calls Italian peasants "primitive" in what seems clearly a pejorative sense.

[19]Addams, "A New Impulse to an Old Gospel," 347; to Henry Demarest

Lloyd, October 18, 1898, in the Lloyd Papers at the State Historical Society of Wisconsin; *The Spirit of Youth*, 28.

[20]Addams, *Philanthropy and Social Progress*, 37; *Newer Ideals of Peace*, 75–76; "Recent Immigration," in the *Education Review*, 29:254–256 (March, 1905); "Chicago Settlements and Social Unrest," in *Charities and the Commons*, 20:165–166 (May 2, 1908).

[21]Addams, "Recent Immigration," 252–260.

[22]Addams, *Democracy and Social Ethics*, 192, 226–227, 252–255; "Ethical Survival in Municipal Corruption," in the *International Journal of Ethics*, 8:276 (April, 1898).

[23]Addams, "Reaction of Moral Instruction on Social Reform," 18; *Newer Ideals of Peace*, 32–33; Address at the Memorial Exercises for Henry Demarest Lloyd, November 29, 1903, p. 12, in the Swarthmore College Peace Collection.

[24]Addams, "Trades Unions and Public Duty," 462; "Subtle Problems of Charity," 177–178.

[25]Addams, *Democracy and Social Ethics*, 2, 3, and *passim*; "Charity and Social Justice," 68, 78; "A Challenge to the Contemporary Church," 198; "Housing Problems in Chicago," in the *Annals of the American Academy of Political and Social Science*, 20:99–107 (July, 1902); "Public Recreation and Social Morality," 494; "Probation Work Under Civil Service," in *Charities*, 15: 881–882 (March, 1906).

[26]Addams, "The Humanitarian Value of Civil Service," in *Survey*, 28: 14–16 (April 6, 1912); "Charity and Social Justice," 69; "A New Impulse to an Old Gospel," 345, 350; "Chicago Settlements and Social Unrest," 155–166.

[27]Addams, *Democracy and Social Ethics*, 276; "A New Impulse to an Old Gospel," 352; "Subtle Problems of Charity," 166–167; "Pragmatism in Politics," in *Survey*, 29:12 (October, 1912). I have used the feminine pronoun because Miss Addams always thought of charity workers in that gender.

[28]Addams, "The College Woman and the Family Claim," in *The Commons*, 29:3 (September, 1898); *Democracy and Social Ethics*, 110.

[29]Addams, "Charity and Social Justice," 69–70; *The Spirit of Youth*, 109; *Democracy and Social Ethics*, 179.

[30]*Ibid.*, 89.

[31]Addams, "The Significance of Organized Labor," an address delivered before the Women's Clubs Convention, Denver, Colorado, 1898 [?], in the Addams Correspondence; "Trade Unions and Public Duty," 459.

[32]Addams, "One Menace to the Century's Progress," an address delivered before the Sunset Club, Chicago, February 14, 1901, in the Swarthmore College Peace Collection; "Problems of Municipal Administration," 427; *Newer Ideals of Peace*, 34–35; "The Significance of Organized Labor"; "Recent Immigration," 246, 263; *Democracy and Social Ethics*, 222–223; *Newer Ideals of Peace*, 87–89; "Ethical Survival in Municipal Corruption: A Chicago Example," in the *Review of Reviews*, 17:605–606 (May, 1898); "Why the Ward Boss Rules," in *Outlook*, 58:879–882 (April, 1898); "Ten Years Experience in Illinois," in the *Annals of the American Academy of Political and Social Sciences*, 38 (supplement) :144–148 (July, 1911); "Charity and Social Justice,"

70; "Trade Unions and Public Duty," 450.

[33]Addams, *Newer Ideals of Peace*, 42, 62, 84, 86; "Problems of Municipal Administration," 432, 437; *Democracy and Social Ethics*, 266–267; "Trades Unions and Public Duty," 448; Robert H. Bremner, *From the Depths* (New York, 1956), 123–140.

[34]Addams, "Charity and Social Justice," 72–73; *Spirit of Youth*, 7; *A New Conscience*, 124, 126; "Pragmatism in Politics," 12. In spite of the large function she favored for government, she insisted that she was not a socialist, which party she accused of taking "refuge in the formulae of a new scholasticism." See *Newer Ideals of Peace*, 86.

[35]Addams, "A New Impulse to an Old Gospel," 353; "Reaction of Modern Life Upon Religious Education," 23, 24, 26; "Reaction of Moral Instruction on Social Reform," 18; "A Modern Lear," 135; *Democracy and Social Ethics*, 2–3, 7, 75, and *passim*.

[36]For an interesting more recent expression of similar ideas, see Erich Fromm, *The Sane Society* (New York, 1955). Social critics such as David Riesman and William H. Whyte have, fifty years after Miss Addams put forth the idea of a social ethic, been pointing out hazards of that ethic. A juxtaposed reading of Addams and Riesman clearly illustrates how solutions to one set of problems may create a new and entirely unsuspected set of problems. Among many other items, compare Riesman's "Their Tribe and Ours," a review of Dorothy Lee's *Freedom and Culture* (New York, 1960), in *The New Republic*, 142:15–16 (February, 1960).

Chapter 2: Samuel Gompers

[1]The biographical section of this chapter is based on Samuel Gompers, *Seventy Years of Life and Labor* (2 vols., New York, 1925); Foster R. Dulles, *Labor in America, A History* (New York, 1949); Joseph G. Rayback, *A History of American Labor* (New York, 1959); Arthur Mann, "Gompers and the Irony of Racism," in the *Antioch Review*, 13:203–214 (Summer, 1953); Phillip A. Taft, *The A. F. of L. in the Time of Gompers* (New York, 1957).

[2]John R. Commons, "Karl Marx and Samuel Gompers," in the *Political Science Quarterly*, 41:281–286 (June, 1926); Gompers to John Elliot, November 1, 1892. Unless otherwise noted, Gompers' letters are cited from his letter books in the American Federation of Labor and Congress of Industrial Organizations Headquarters in Washington; *American Federationist*, 4:114 (August, 1897). Unless otherwise indicated, references to this journal refer to the editorials that Gompers wrote. Marc Karson, in his *American Labor Movement and Politics, 1900–1918* (Carbondale, Illinois, 1958), seems to think that Gompers' class consciousness declined after about 1900.

[3]Gompers to Frank M. Notton, December 2, 1893, where he speaks of capitalists as "our natural enemies"; Gompers to P. J. McGuire, November 4, 1892; *American Federationist*, 1:99 (July, 1894); 8:215 (June, 1901); 8:479 (November, 1901); 7:165 (June, 1900); 8:363 (September, 1901); 4:214

(November, 1897); 1:98 (July, 1894); 9:179 (April, 1902); Gompers, "Judicial Invasion of Guaranteed Rights," in the *American Federationist*, 17:298 (April, 1910).

[4]*Ibid.*, 7:134 (May, 1900); 8:314 (October, 1900); 8:358 (September, 1901); 9:71 (February, 1902); 7:165 (June, 1900); 7:246 (August, 1900); Gompers to Emil Applehagen, September 11, 1890. See also Gompers' testimony in National Industrial Commission *Report* (Washington, 1901), 7:598.

[5]*American Federationist*, 9:22 (January, 1902); 7:314 (October, 1900); 11:911 (October, 1904); 19:471 (June, 1912).

[6]*Ibid.*, 10:91 (February, 1903); 11:138 (February, 1904); Gompers to Henry Demarest Lloyd, March 15, 1898, in the Lloyd Papers.

[7]Gompers, "Ministers Debate Labor," in the *American Federationist*, 9:438–440 (August, 1902). Frequently Gompers said that while a man might burn down his house on an open prairie, he could not do so in a crowded city. Fellowship begat responsibilities which limited freedom.

[8]American Federation of Labor, *Report of Proceedings of the Twelfth Annual Convention of the American Federation of Labor*, 1892, p. 12. Hereafter cited as *Convention Proceedings*, with the year. *Convention Proceedings*, 1894, p. 21.

[9]*American Federationist*, 7:283–284 (September, 1900); *Convention Proceedings*, 1890, p. 17; *American Federationist*, 8:317–318 (October, 1900); *Convention Proceedings*, 1900, p. 21; *American Federationist*, 15:203 (March, 1908). See also Gompers' testimony in National Industrial Commission *Report* (Washington, 1901), 7:600–604, 612–613.

[10]Louis S. Reed, *The Labor Philosophy of Samuel Gompers* (New York, 1930), 97–103; Gompers to Dennis J. Bulkly, September 13, 1900; Gompers, "Organized Labor in the Campaign of 1892," in the *North American Review*, 155:91–96 (July, 1892); *Convention Proceedings*, 1891, p. 15; *American Federationist*, 5:54 (May, 1898); 5:115 (August, 1898).

[11]*Convention Proceedings*, 1892, p. 13; *ibid.*, 1893, p. 12; Gompers to Henry Miller, April 14, 1893; Gompers to A. J. Oliver, April 19, 1893; Gompers to J. W. Sullivan, May 17, 1892; *Convention Proceedings*, 1906, p. 32; *American Federationist*, 15:126 (February, 1908); 15:341–354 (April, 1908); 11:33 (January, 1904); 19:140 (February, 1912); 19:217 (March, 1912).

[12]*Ibid.*, 15:180–192 (March, 1908); 15:276–279 (April, 1908); 15:457 (June, 1908).

[13]*Ibid.*, 15:527–528 (July, 1908); 15:598 (August, 1908); 19:801 (October, 1912); 19:889–894 (August, 1912). Undoubtedly Gompers' coolness toward the Bull Moose party grew out of a suspicion of a party which drew most of its strength from the Republicans. He was perhaps unwilling to hitch labor's wagon to a new and possibly temporary star, and he was less than enthusiastic about Theodore Roosevelt. Certainly of equal importance, however, must have been ideological considerations. Roosevelt's centralism, nationalism, and paternalism were incompatible with Gompers' essentially laissez-faire instincts which fitted far more easily into Woodrow Wilson's New Freedom.

[14]*Ibid.*, 9:69 (February, 1902); 18:243 (March, 1910).

[15]*Ibid.*, 17:41 (January, 1910); "President Gompers in Europe," in *ibid.*, 17:146, 241 (February, March, 1910); *ibid.*, 14:215–216 (November, 1897); 5:179–183 (November, 1898); 5:204 (December, 1898); 7:36 (April, 1899); Gompers to Lloyd, October 13, 1890, in the Lloyd Papers. Gompers, along with most European socialists, abandoned this view under the pressure of World War I. The mechanism of this process is complex, ill understood, and in any case beyond the scope of this study.

[16]Gompers to Callahan, May 17, 1892; to Norton, May 16 and 17, 1892; to Frederick J. Carr, December 8, 1891; *American Federationist*, 1:50–51 (May, 1894); 12:833 (November, 1905); 8:362 (September, 1901); 9:125 (March, 1902); 8:480 (November, 1901); 8:305–306 (August, 1901); 9:70 (February, 1902); compare Bernard Mandel, "Samuel Gompers and the Negro Worker," in the *Journal of Negro History*, 40:34–60 (January, 1955).

[17]*Convention Proceedings*, 1900, p. 23; *American Federationist*, 8:118–120 (April, 1901); 12:636–637 (September, 1905).

[18]Gompers' speech at Lawrence, Massachusetts, quoted in the *American Federationist*, 12:371 (June, 1905); speech at Omaha, in *ibid.*, 12:451 (July, 1905); speech in Washington, in *ibid.*, 12:147 (March, 1905); see also, *ibid.*, 12:75 (February, 1905); 12:449 (July, 1905); 19:101–114 (February, 1912).

[19]*Ibid.*, 10:830 (September, 1903); 18:297 (April, 1910); 19:372 (May, 1912); 6:33 (April, 1899); 17:146 (February, 1910); 5:70 (June, 1898); 17:489 (June, 1910); 7:103 (April, 1900); Gompers to A. M. Haefeld, April 17, 1893.

[20]Gompers to John B. Lennon, August 11, 1890; to F. W. Gilwreath, August 19, 1891; to George S. Burleson, August 22, 1891; *Convention Proceedings*, 1891, p. 3.

[21]Gompers to Mrs. T. J. Morgan, September 10, 1891; *American Federationist*, 6:248 (December, 1899).

[22]For one example of many where Gompers refused to aid a union in arrears on its per-capita tax, see Gompers to J. T. Joyce, Richmond, Indiana, June 26, 1893. A statement favoring a small militant group, rather than a large loose one is in Gompers to Lloyd, April 18, 1892, in the Lloyd Papers.

[23]*American Federationist*, 15:460 (April, 1908); 4:96 (July, 1897); 7:100–101 (April, 1900).

[24]*Ibid.*, 17:32 (April, 1910); 7:10 (January, 1900); 6:81 (June, 1899); 6:10 (January, 1900); 7:81 (June, 1899); *Convention Proceedings*, 1893, p. 37; New York *Times*, August 21, 1893.

[25]See for example Gompers' testimony in National Industrial Commission *Report* (Washington, 1901), 7:645.

Chapter 3: The Civic Federation Of Chicago

[1]Harold C. Syrett, *The City of Brooklyn, 1865–1898* (New York, 1944); Donald W. Disbrow, The Progressive Movement in Philadelphia, unpublished Ph.D. dissertation, University of Rochester, 1957, pp. 327–329; Ransom W. Noble, *New Jersey Progressivism before Wilson* (Princeton, 1946); William

D. Miller, *The Progressive Movement in Memphis* (Memphis, 1957), especially p. 178; Walton Bean, *Boss Reuf's San Francisco* (Berkeley, 1952), 28–55; James B. Whipple, Cleveland in Conflict, a Study in Urban Adolescence, unpublished Ph.D. dissertation, Western Reserve University, 1951; Tom L. Johnson, *My Story* (New York, 1913), 125–131.

²Civic Federation of Chicago, *Civic Federation of Chicago* (Chicago, 1894). This is a pamphlet containing the charter and by-laws. See also, *First Annual Report of the Central Council, 1894–1895* (Chicago, 1895), 7, 10–11.

³*Ibid.*, 9.

⁴*Ibid.*, 7, 10.

⁵*Ibid.*, 32, 38.

⁶*Ibid.*, 28, 33–36.

⁷*Ibid.*, 35.

⁸Descriptions of Chicago's ribald politics are legion; for particularly dramatic pictures, see Carter H. Harrison, *Stormy Years* (Indianapolis, 1935); Lloyd Wendt and Herman Kogan, *Lords of the Levee; The Story of Bath House John and Hinky Dink* (Indianapolis, 1943); Elizabeth Kent, *William Kent, Independent* (n.p., [1950?]).

⁹Douglas Sutherland, *Fifty Years on the Civic Front* (Chicago, 1943), 11–12, 16; Chicago *Tribune,* January 7, 1898, p. 10; Civic Federation of Chicago, *First Annual Report,* 8, 62.

¹⁰*Ibid.*, 14; William K. Ackerman, *Report of Investigation into the Affairs of the Street Railways of Chicago, made to the Civic Federation* (Chicago, 1898); Civic Federation of Chicago, *The Street Railways of Chicago* (Chicago, 1901), 1–48.

¹¹Civic Federation of Chicago, *First Annual Report,* 41–42.

¹²E. Allen Frost, Robert McCurdy, and Harry S. Mecartney, *Chicago and the Constitution, Report to the Civic Federation* (Chicago, 1902), 25–26; Sutherland, *Fifty Years,* 23–24; Civic Federation of Chicago, *Bi-ennial Report for 1905* (Chicago, [1905?]), 5–6.

¹³University of Illinois, *Illinois State Revenue, 1895–1920* (Urbana, 1922); Robert M. Haig, *A History of the General Property Tax in Illinois* (Urbana, 1914); John A. Farlie, *A Report on the Taxation and Revenue System of Illinois prepared for the Special Tax Commission of the State of Illinois* (Danville, 1910); Sutherland, *Fifty Years,* 38–40; Civic Federation of Chicago, *Tax Inequities in Illinois* (Chicago, [1910?]); the Federation here was much closer to the views of the Founding Fathers than it was to those of the reformers demanding greater popular participation in government. The question of strong leadership is more complex, however. Some of the leading philosophers of reform favored strong leadership not as a check on the popular will, but as an inspiration for it. See Charles Forcey, *Crossroads of Liberalism* (New York, 1961).

¹⁴Civic Federation of Chicago, *Dangers of the Initiative and Referendum* (Chicago, [1911?]); *Bi-ennial Report, 1911,* (Chicago, [1911?]).

[15]Lloyd Lewis and Henry Justin Smith, *Chicago, The History of Its Reputation* (New York, 1929), 237; Sutherland, *Fifty Years*, 10, 11, 87; Civic Federation of Chicago, *First Annual Report*, 17–18, 49–54; *Analysis of Chicago Market Milk* (Chicago, 1904); *Bi-ennial Report, 1905* (Chicago, [1905?]), 16–19; Senate Document no. 133, vol. 3, 59 Congress, 1 Session, serial 4911; Civic Federation of Chicago, *Saving Lives with Pictures* (Chicago, [1910?]); *Bi-ennial Report, 1907* (Chicago, [1907?]), 9–10; *Bi-ennial Report, 1911; Legislative Report* (Chicago, 1911), cover.

[16]Graham Taylor, *Pioneering on Social Frontiers* (Chicago, 1930), 31–32.

[17]Civic Federation of Chicago, *National Conference on Industrial Conciliation* (Chicago, 1894); Chicago *Daily News*, November 13, 14, 15, 1894, pp. 1, 1, and 4; Civic Federation of Chicago, *First Annual Report*, 78–81; Frost *et al.*, *Chicago and the Constitution*, 25–26.

[18]Civic Federation of Chicago, *Legislative Report*, 10–12.

[19]Harrison, *Stormy Years*, 138.

[20]Lyman Gage considered the business cycle to be a simple, natural, periodic occurrence; see his *Memoirs* (New York, 1937), 65–67.

[21]Joseph Flinn, *Handbook of Chicago Biography* (Chicago, 1893); John W. Leonard, *A Book of Chicagoans* (Chicago, 1905); *Chicago City Directory*, 1911.

[22]Wendt and Kogan, *Lords of the Levee;* Harrison, *Stormy Years*, 129; Howard Zink, *City Bosses in the United States* (Durham, N. C., 1930). In a sense Jane Addams tried to use her beneficence to buy back the voters to virtue, away from the beneficence of the ward boss.

[23]Ray Stannard Baker, "The Civic Federation of Chicago," in *Outlook*, 52:132 (July, 1895); Albion W. Small, "The Civic Federation of Chicago," in the *American Journal of Sociology*, 1:79–103 (July, 1895); Taylor, *Pioneering on Social Frontiers*, 33–59; Lewis and Smith, *Chicago*, 243.

CHAPTER 4: ALBERT J. BEVERIDGE

[1]The standard biography is Claude G. Bowers, *Beveridge and the Progressive Era* (New York, 1932). See also Charles F. Remy, "The Election of Beveridge to the Senate," in the *Indiana Magazine of History*, 36:123–135 (June, 1940); John Braeman, "The Rise of Albert J. Beveridge to the United States Senate," in *ibid.*, 53:355–382 (December, 1957).

[2]Beveridge to Charles G. Dawes, May 10, 1898, Letter book, in the Beveridge Papers in the Library of Congress.

[3]John Higham, *Strangers in the Land* (New Brunswick, N. J., 1955), 131–144, 149–157; Richard Hofstadter, *Social Darwinism in American Thought* (Boston, 1955), 170–201; George E. Mowry, *The Era of Theodore Roosevelt* (New York, 1958), 92–94; Beveridge to John Temple Graves, January 26, 1900, Letter book, in the Beveridge Papers. Beveridge was as loose as his contemporaries in his definition of the term "race."

[4]*Congressional Record*, 56 Congress, 1 session, part 1, p. 711 (January 9, 1900); Beveridge, "Conservatism: The Spirit of National Self-Restraint," a

speech delivered on February 22, 1902, in Chicago, in Albert J. Beveridge, *The Meaning of the Times and other Speeches* (Indianapolis, 1908), 156; "True Liberty Under Law," in *The Reader*, 10:149 (July, 1907); "National Integrity," in *ibid.*, 7:570–571.

⁵Beveridge, *The Russian Advance* (New York, 1903), 176. See also, *ibid.*, pp. 34, 47, 283. "Our Canadian Cousins: How They Handle Their Immigration Problems," in the *Saturday Evening Post*, August 26, 1911, p. 9; *Congressional Record*, 56 Congress, 1 session, part 8, Appendix, pp. 285–292 (June 3, 1902).

⁶Beveridge to Larz A. Whitcomb, March 7, 1900, Letter book, in the Beveridge Papers; *The Russian Advance*, 16; *Congressional Record*, 59 Congress, 1 session, part 4, pp. 3522–3523 (March 8, 1906).

⁷Beveridge, "Business and Government," a speech delivered in Chicago on September 22, 1906, in *The Meaning of the Times*, 269; "The Star of Empire," a speech delivered in Chicago on September 25, 1900, in *ibid.*, 118; "Forefathers' Day," a speech delivered in St. Louis on December 21, 1896, in *ibid.*, 24; "Conservatism, The Spirit of National Self-Restraint," 153; manuscript of speech, "Heroism and the Law," [1893?], in the Beveridge Papers; "The College Man in Politics," manuscript of speech delivered to DKE fraternity November 22, 25, 1897, in *ibid.*; "Development of a Colonial Policy," in the *Annals of the American Academy of Political and Social Sciences*, 30:12 (July, 1907).

⁸Beveridge, *The Russian Advance*, 33–39, 40, 43, 19–20, 338–366, 426–461; *The Bible as Good Reading* (Philadelphia, 1904), 19–29, 65–79.

⁹Albeit Cleveland was not a candidate in 1896.

¹⁰Manuscript of "Altgeld Speech," delivered in Chicago on October 29, 1896, in the Beveridge Papers.

¹¹Beveridge, "Government of Dependencies," in *The Reader*, 10:260 (August, 1907); "Nation," in *ibid.*, 9:356–358 (March, 1907); "Vitality of the American Constitution," a speech delivered in Pittsburgh on January 4, 1898, in *The Meaning of the Times*, 6–10. This point of view is emphasized in Beveridge's biographies of Lincoln and Marshall; see *Abraham Lincoln* (2 vols., New York, 1928); *The Life of John Marshall* (4 vols., New York, 1916–1919); "State and Nation," a speech delivered in Galena, Illinois, on April 27, 1907, in *The Meaning of the Times*, 404–419; "Federalism in Canada and in the United States," in the *Review of Reviews*, 44:471–476 (October, 1911); "Our Canadian Cousins: The History of a Railroad Triumvirate," in the *Saturday Evening Post*, July 22, 1911, pp. 10–12, 32–33; manuscript of speech, "Reply to Mr. Bryan," [1901?], in the Beveridge Papers.

¹²Beveridge, "The Organization of American Business," a speech opening the Republican campaign in Colorado, 1902, in *The Meaning of the Times*, 184; "Our Canadian Cousins: How They Handle Their Currency Problems," in the *Saturday Evening Post*, June 17, 1911, p. 4; "Trusts and their Treatment," in *The Reader*, 10:40–46 (June, 1907); "Regulation not Extermination," in *ibid.*, 9:579–588 (May, 1907).

¹³Beveridge, "Mutual Confidence and Consideration," in *The Reader*,

10:380–381 (September, 1907); manuscript of speech, "The Relation of the State to Labor," (misdated 1900, but probably 1905), in the Beveridge Papers.

[14]Beveridge, "Development of a Colonial Policy," 4–5; *The Russian Advance*, 12, 122–137. Compare Richard Hofstadter, *Social Darwinism in American Thought*, especially pp. 143–201; Beveridge to Graves, March 12, 1901, in the Beveridge Papers; manuscript of a speech, "The Young Men of America," delivered at a Republican meeting in Indianapolis on October 18, 1900, in *ibid.*; "The Command of the Pacific," a speech delivered in San Francisco on September 15, 1902, in *The Meaning of the Times*, 189–197; "True Liberty Under the Law," 10.

[15]Beveridge, manuscript of a speech "Memorial Oration," delivered on May 30, 1892, at Mount Vernon, Indiana, in the Beveridge Papers.

[16]Beveridge, "A Permanent Tariff Commission," in the *Annals of the American Academy of Political and Social Sciences*, 32:421–422 (September, 1908); "The Insurgents," in the *Saturday Evening Post*, October 16, 1909, p. 4; "Our Canadian Cousins: Profiting by Our Mistakes," in *ibid.*, September 9, 1911, p. 26; *The Russian Advance*, 11, 183, 322.

[17]*Congressional Record*, 56 Congress, 1 session, part 1, p. 711 (January 9, 1900); *ibid.*, part 8, Appendix, p. 281 (March 29, 1900); Beveridge, "Vitality of the American Constitution," in *The Meaning of the Times*, 11–19; to Robert J. Tracewell, September 30, 1908, in the Beveridge Papers; to the Hon. George B. Cardwell, July 13, 1898, in *ibid.*

[18]Beveridge, "Conservatism: The Spirit of National Self-Restraint," in *The Meaning of the Times*, 157; "Duties of the Present; Not Memories of the Past," a speech delivered on November 3, 1906, in Indianapolis, in *ibid.*, 295–296; "Business and Government," in *ibid.*, 271–272.

[19]Beveridge, "The Command of the Pacific," in *ibid.*, 189; "The College Man in Politics," in the Beveridge Papers; "Our Canadian Cousins. Profiting By Our Mistakes," in the *Saturday Evening Post*, September 9, 1911, p. 27; *The Young Man and the World* (New York, 1911), 15–16, 19–20, 83, 113; to George W. Perkins, June 6, 1898, in the Beveridge Papers.

[20]"Speech for 1892 Campaign," in the Beveridge Papers. This is a manuscript of a speech that was presumably delivered several times during the campaign. Beveridge, *The Young Man and the World*, 118. This book, issued in 1911, stands in direct contradiction to the statements quoted below.

[21]Beveridge to David Graham Phillips, August 1, 1906, in the Beveridge Papers; manuscript, "Speech at Mounds Park, Indiana, July 4, 1910," in *ibid.*; keynote speech at the Progressive Party Convention, Chicago. The text appears in full in the Chicago *Daily News*, August 5, 1912.

[22]Beveridge to John C. Shaffer, January 26, [1900?]; to Lorimer, February 3, 1900, Letter books; to Graves, January 26, 1900; to Phillips, November 15, 1908, all in the Beveridge Papers.

[23]"Speech for 1892 Campaign"; "Speech for 1902 Campaign"; and manuscript of a speech, "All is Well with the Republic," all in *ibid.*

[24]Beveridge, "Progressive Liberty," a speech delivered on April 11, 1906,

in Indianapolis, in *The Meaning of the Times,* 263; to Phillips, April 18, 1906, in the Beveridge Papers; to Roosevelt, May 27, 1908, in *ibid.;* "Campaign Speech No. 2, 1910"; "Campaign Speech, 1911," both in *ibid.;* "Our Canadian Cousins: How They Break Their Trusts to Harness," in the *Saturday Evening Post,* July 1, 1911, pp. 10–11, 44–45; to Roosevelt, November 16, 1910, in the Beveridge Papers; to Phillips, November 19, 1910, in *ibid.* In 1922 he returned to a more orthodox version of Republicanism when he campaigned unsuccessfully for the Senate. See Bowers, *Beveridge,* 509–513, 526–535.

²⁵Beveridge to William Loeb, November 9, 1906, in the Beveridge Papers.

Chapter 5: Edgar Gardner Murphy

¹The biographical section of this chapter is based on Maude K. Murphy, *Edgar Gardner Murphy* (New York, 1943); correspondence with Murphy's two sons, Gardner Murphy of the Menninger Clinic, Topeka, Kansas, and Reverend Du Bose Murphy of Tuscaloosa, Alabama; Herbert J. Doherty, Jr., "Voices of Protest from the New South," in the *Mississippi Valley Historical Review,* 42:45–66 (June, 1955); Allen J. Going, "The Reverend Edgar Gardner Murphy, His Ideas and Influence," in the *Historical Magazine of the Protestant Episcopal Church,* 25:391–402 (December, 1956); C. Vann Woodward, *Origins of the New South* (Baton Rouge, 1951).

²Edgar Gardner Murphy, *The Basis of Ascendancy* (New York, 1909), 149; "The Task of the Leader," in the *Sewanee Review,* 15:14 (January, 1907).

³Murphy, "Backward or Forward?" in the *South Atlantic Quarterly,* 8:27–28 (January, 1909); *The Basis of Ascendancy,* 30–31. These are his words. He meant that the differences between whites and Negroes could not be eliminated. "Reconstruction in Religion," in *The Outlook,* 47:682 (March, 1901).

⁴Murphy, *Problems of the Present South* (New York, 1910).

⁵Murphy, *The Basis of Ascendancy,* 150, 175–177, 200.

⁶*Ibid.,* 8, 186, 193–194.

⁷Murphy, "The Task of the Leader," 12.

⁸An undated letter from Murphy to the editor of the Montgomery *Advertiser,* in the Murphy Papers in the Southern Historical Collection of the University of North Carolina, Chapel Hill; *Problems of the Present South,* 38–42, 66.

⁹Murphy, *The White Man and the Negro at the South* (n.p., 1900), 33; "Shall the Fourteenth Amendment be Enforced?" in the *North American Review,* 180:109–133 (January, 1905); to Felix Adler, May 27, 1907; to the New York *Post,* May 2, 1903, both in the Murphy Papers; *Federal Regulation of Child Labor* (n.p., 1907); *The South and Her Children* (n.p., 1903); *The Peonage Cases in Alabama* (n.p., 1903); *Child Labor in Alabama* (n.p., 1901).

¹⁰Murphy, *The Basis of Ascendancy,* xvi, 77, 79, 85–89; *Problems of the Present South,* 34.

[11]*Ibid.*, 46; *The Basis of Ascendancy*, xv, 40–43, 12–14. Compare Melville J. Herskowitz, *The Myth of the Negro Past* (New York, 1941); Murphy to Clay Lilly, March 30, 1903, Letter books, in the Murphy Papers.

[12]Murphy, *The White Man and the Negro*, 19; *The Basis of Ascendancy*, 107–108; *Problems of the Present South*, 34, 63. The proponents of South African *appartheid* have now made such arguments a disguise for cruelty. This, however, was not Murphy's aim.

[13]*Ibid.*, 63; Murphy, "The Task of the Leader," 11; *The Basis of Ascendancy*, 223, 111; to Jane Addams, November 7, 1909, in the Addams Papers.

[14]Murphy, "Shall the Fourteenth Amendment Be Enforced?" *passim*, but especially pp. 121–122; "The Task of the Leader," 22–24.

[15]Murphy, *The Basis of Ascendancy*, 10, 11, 30–32, 59–60, 161, 121–127.

[16]Murphy to Booker T. Washington, July 17, July 27, 1909, in the Washington Papers at the Library of Congress.

[17]Murphy, *The Basis of Ascendancy*, xvii, 9–10, 25–28, 44–48, 56–57, 70–77, 106, 147n, 148; *The Church and the Negro Episcopate* (n.p., 1907), 8, 10–11; *Short Letter on the Southern Question* (n.p., 1907); *Problems of the Present South*, 69–71.

[18]*Ibid.*, 73–74; *The Basis of Ascendancy*, 61–63.

[19]*Ibid.*, 112; *Southern Education in Its National Aspects* (n.p., 1902), 3; *The Church and the Negro Episcopate*, 3.

[20]Murphy, "The Public Function of the Public School," a chapter in the incomplete manuscript for a book to be entitled *Issues Southern and National*, in the Murphy Papers; "The Freedman's Progress in the South," in *The Outlook*, 68: 721–724 (July, 1901); "Shall the Fourteenth Amendment be Enforced?" 126.

[21]Murphy, "Backward or Forward?" 31–34; *Alabama's First Question* (Montgomery, 1902), 2.

[22]Murphy, "Reconstruction in Religion," 682–684; *The Basis of Ascendancy*, 18–19, 100–104; and an undated letter from Murphy to J. D. Barron, in the Murphy Papers.

[23]Murphy, *Problems of the Present South*, 61–62.

[24]Murphy, *The Church and the Negro Episcopate*, 3; "Progress in Southern Education," in *The Tradesman*, January 1, 1908, in the Murphy Papers.

[25]"Democracy and Culture," a speech delivered on June 24, 1903, at the University of the South, in the Murphy Papers.

[26]Murphy, "The Task of the Leader," 1–30.

CHAPTER 6: ROBERT M. LA FOLLETTE

[1]The biographical section of this chapter is based on Robert M. La Follette, *Autobiography* (Madison, 1913); Belle C. La Follette and Fola La Follette, *Robert M. La Follette* (2 vols., New York, 1953); Robert S. Maxwell, *La Follette and the Rise of the Progressives in Wisconsin* (Madison, 1956), and interviews with Fola La Follette in Washington on February 1, 2, 3, 1960.

[2]Merle Curti and Vernon Carstensen, *The University of Wisconsin* (2 vols., Madison, 1949); John Bascom, *Problems in Philosophy* (New York, 1885), 107.

[3]Maxwell, *La Follette*, 13.

[4]Opening speech of the 1892 campaign, in the La Follette Papers at the State Historical Society of Wisconsin, Madison. The main body of La Follette manuscripts is in the Library of Congress, but is not yet open to scholars. Hereafter reference to La Follette Papers refers to the collection in Madison; *La Follette's Magazine*, 1:4 (January 9, 1909). Unless otherwise indicated references to this magazine are to the editorials, for which La Follette himself was responsible. La Follette, *Autobiography*, 1–17, 22; La Follette to Edward J. Gross, June 28, 1916, in the Gross Papers at the State Historical Society of Wisconsin, in which La Follette described himself as an uncompromising man of principle fighting for free institutions and real democracy. Nevertheless, from his first term as governor of Wisconsin to his election as United States Senator, no veto of his was ever overridden. See Wisconsin *Senate Journal* and *Assembly Journal* for the 1901, 1903, and 1905 sessions.

[5]Undated manuscript speech, [1900?], in the La Follette Papers; La Follette, *Autobiography*, 223–224.

[6]*Ibid.*, 42; *La Follette's Magazine*, 1:4 (April 17, 1909); 1:3 (April 24, 1909); 1:3 (May 8, 1909); undated manuscript speech, [1903?], in the La Follette Papers.

[7]Wisconsin *Senate Journal*, 1901, p. 35.

[8]Undated manuscript speech, [1902?], in the La Follette Papers; *La Follette's Magazine*, 1:4 (August 14, 1909); 3:4, 7 (February 4, 1911).

[9]Undated manuscript speech to Hibernians, [1902?], in the La Follette Papers; *La Follette's Magazine*, 1:4 (May 8, 1909); 3:4 (April 29, 1911); 4:3 (April 6, 1912).

[10]*Ibid.*, 1:5 (October 9, 1909); 11:3 (December 31, 1910); 3:3 (December 2, 1911).

[11]*Ibid.*, 1:5 (March 6, 1909); 1:4 (May 5, 1909).

[12]All from undated manuscript speeches, [1902?], in the La Follette Papers.

[13]*La Follette's Magazine*, 1:4 (September 4, 1909); 2:5 (January 22, 1910); 3:3 (December 16, 1911); 2:3 (October 22, 1910); 3:3 (April 22, 1911); undated manuscript speech, [1893?], in the La Follette Papers; La Follette, *Autobiography*, 41, 223.

[14]*La Follette's Magazine*, 1:6 (February 6, 1909); 1:4 (June 12, 1909); 1:3 (May 5, 1909); 1:4 (March 20, 1909); 1:4–5 (January 30, 1909); 2:4 (January 8, 1910); 2:4 (February 12, 1910); *Congressional Record*, 59 Congress, 1 session, p. 5690 (April 23, 1906); *ibid.*, 61 Congress, 2 session, p. 6906 (May 26, 1910), in which La Follette used "Wall Street" in a pejorative sense; *ibid.*, 62 Congress, 1 session, p. 1963 (June 13, 1911); undated manuscript speeches, [1894–1896?], in the La Follette Papers; Messages to the legislature, 1901, 1903, in Wisconsin *Senate Journal* for those years.

[15]Maxwell, *La Follette*, 56–58; interview with Fola La Follette on Feb-

ruary 1, 1960.

[16]Opening speech, 1892 campaign, in the La Follette Papers; undated manuscript speeches, [1900?], in *ibid.*; *Congressional Record,* 59 Congress, 1 session, p. 5694 (April 23, 1906); *La Follette's Magazine,* 1:3 (January 23, 1909); 2:3–4 (February 5, 1910); 2:3 (March 26, 1910); La Follette to Nicolay Greestead, March 25, 1895, in the La Follette Papers.

[17]Executive Communication, Wisconsin *Senate Journal,* 1905, pp. 1207–1212; La Follette to Greestead, March 25, 1895, in the La Follette Papers; to A. R. Hall, November 14, 1894, in the Hall Papers at the State Historical Society of Wisconsin; *La Follette's Magazine,* 2:3 (May 21, 1910); 2:3 (April 30, 1910).

[18]*Ibid.,* 1:4 (August 21, 1909); 1:3–4 (April 3, 1909); 2:3 (June 25, 1910); 2:3 (August 13, 1910); 4:3 (February 3, 1912); 3:3, 7 (April 29, 1911); 4:3 (April 13, 1912).

[19]*Ibid.,* 1:3 (March 13, 1909); La Follette, *Autobiography,* 67, 186; undated manuscript speech, [1898?], in the La Follette Papers.

[20]*La Follette's Magazine,* 3:3–4 (May 27, 1911); 3:12 (February 4, 1911); 1:4 (February 27, 1909); 1:4 (February 13, 1909); 3:3 (March 25, 1911); 1:3 (December 11, 1909); La Follette, *Autobiography,* 125, 244. Wilson opposed the use of scientific experts; see his *A Crossroads of Freedom,* edited by John W. Davidson (New Haven, 1956), 160–161, 163.

[21]Undated manuscript speech, [1902?], in the La Follette Papers; *La Follette's Magazine,* 50:5 (March 6, 1909); 1:5 (December 4, 1909).

[22]La Follette, *Autobiography,* 270.

[23]Robert La Follette to Belle C. La Follette, January 28, 1907, quoted in Belle C. and Fola La Follette, *Robert M. La Follette,* 222; to Theodore Roosevelt, February 19, 1907, quoted in *ibid.,* 223; La Follette, *Autobiography,* 268; *Congressional Record,* 59 Congress, 1 session, pp. 5690, 5695–5697, 5700–5701 (April 23, 1906); *ibid.,* 61 Congress, 2 session, pp. 4560–4563 (April 12, 1910), 7372–7374 (June 3, 1910), 6882–6883 (May 26, 1910).

[24]Maxwell, *La Follette,* 10–40; Robert M. La Follette to Belle C. La Follette, January 11, 1907, quoted in Belle C. and Fola La Follette, *Robert M. La Follette,* 219.

[25]Interview with Fola La Follette, February 1 and 2, 1960; *La Follette's Magazine,* 2:4 (April 2, 1910), in which La Follette recommended Jane Addams' autobiography; undated manuscript speech, [1900?], in the La Follette Papers; message to the legislature, 1901, in the Wisconsin *Senate Journal,* 1901, p. 39; undated manuscript speech, [1905?], in the La Follette Papers; Executive Communication, in the Wisconsin *Senate Journal,* 1905, pp. 834–841, 1304–1306, 1421–1425; *Congressional Record,* 61 Congress, 2 session, pp. 6882, 6883 (May 26, 1910); *ibid.,* 59 Congress, 1 session, p. 5702; Maxwell, *La Follette,* 153–164; Charles McCarthy, *The Wisconsin Idea* (New York, 1912), 156–171.

[26]*La Follette's Magazine,* 1:3 (July 31, 1909); 1:3 (October 23, 1909);

2:3 (January 8, 1910); 1:5 (August 28, 1909); 1:3 (July 17, 1909); 4:3–4 (January 13, 1912); 4:3 (February 24, 1912); 1:13 (February 20, 1909); 3:3 (May 20, 1911); 2:3–4 (April 30, 1910).

[27]*Congressional Record*, 62 Congress, 1 session, pp. 4183–4184 (August 19, 1911); Wisconsin *Senate Journal*, 1901, p. 45, where La Follette draws a clear distinction between bigness, which he does not oppose, and monopoly, which he does. He did, however, want government to maintain competition, not control the terms of monopoly; see *Congressional Record*, 59 Congress, 1 session, p. 9093 (June 25, 1906).

Bibliography

PRIMARY SOURCES: MANUSCRIPT COLLECTIONS

a. AFL-CIO Headquarters, Washington.
    Samuel Gompers Papers

b. Library of Congress, Washington.
    Albert J. Beveridge Papers
    Sophonisba Breckinridge Papers
    Theodore Roosevelt Papers
    William Allen White Papers
    Booker T. Washington Papers

c. Southern History Collection, University of North Carolina, Chapel Hill.
    Edgar Gardner Murphy Papers

d. State Historical Society of Wisconsin, Madison.
    Joseph D. Beck Papers
    Charles R. Boardman Papers
    Bryan J. Castle Papers
    Henry A. Cooper Papers
    Edward J. Gross Papers
    A. R. Hall Papers
    Ada James Papers
    Robert M. La Follette Papers
    Henry Demarest Lloyd Papers
    Raymond Robbins Papers
    E. A. Ross Papers
    James A. Stone Papers
    John M. Whitehead Papers

e. Swarthmore College Peace Collection, Swarthmore, Pennsylvania.
    Jane Addams Correspondence

PRIMARY SOURCES: BOOKS

Addams, Jane. *Democracy and Social Ethics.* New York, 1902.
.... *Newer Ideals of Peace.* New York, 1907.
.... *The Spirit of Youth in the City Streets.* New York, 1909.
.... *Twenty Years at Hull House.* New York, 1910.

.... *A New Conscience and an Ancient Evil.* New York, 1912.

Bascom, John. *Problems in Philosophy.* New York, 1885.

Beveridge, Albert J. *The Russian Advance.* New York, 1903.

.... *The Bible as Good Reading.* Philadelphia, 1907.

.... *Americans of Today and Tomorrow.* Philadelphia, 1908.

.... *The Meaning of the Times and Other Speeches.* Indianapolis, 1908.

.... *The Young Man and the World.* New York, 1911.

Gage, Lyman J. *Memoirs of Lyman Gage.* New York, 1937.

Harrison, Carter H. *Stormy Years.* Indianapolis, 1935.

Johnson, Tom L. *My Story.* New York, 1913.

La Follette, Robert M. *The Autobiography of Robert M. La Follette.* New York, 1912.

Murphy, Edgar Gardner. *The Basis of Ascendancy.* New York, 1909.

.... *Problems of the Present South.* New York, 1910.

Older, Fremont. *My Own Story.* New York, 1926.

Roosevelt, Theodore. *Works.* National Edition, New York, 1926.

Taylor, Graham. *Pioneering on Social Frontiers.* Chicago, 1930.

Whitlock, Brand. *Forty Years of It.* New York, 1914.

Wilson, Woodrow. *A Crossroads of Freedom.* Edited by John W. Davidson. New Haven, 1956.

PRIMARY SOURCES: ARTICLES

a. Articles by Jane Addams.

"A Belated Industry." *American Journal of Sociology,* 1:536–550 (March, 1896).

"A New Impulse to an Old Gospel." *Forum,* 14:345–358 (November, 1892).

"Bad Boy of the Streets." *Ladies Home Journal,* 26:17 (October, 1909).

"Charity and Social Justice." *North American Review,* 192:68–81 (July, 1910).

"Charity Visitors Perplexities." *Outlook,* 61:598–600 (March, 1899).

"Chicago Settlements and Social Unrest." *Charities,* 20:155–166 (May, 1908).

"Child Labor and Pauperism." *Charities,* 11:300–304 (October, 1903).

"Child Labor on the Stage." *Annals of the American Academy of Political and Social Sciences,* 38:60–65 (Supplement, July, 1911).

"College Women and Christianity." *Independent,* 53:182–185 (August, 1901).

"Ethical Survival in Municipal Corruption." *International Journal of Ethics,* 8:197–209 (April, 1898).

"Failure of the Modern City to Provide Recreation for Young Girls." *Charities,* 21:365–368 (December, 1908).

"Housing Problems in Chicago." *Annals of the American Academy of Political and Social Sciences,* 20:99–107 (July, 1902).

"Hull House, Chicago; An Effort Toward Social Democracy." *Forum,* 14:226–241 (October, 1892).

"Humanizing Tendency of Industrial Education." *Chautauqua Magazine,* 39:266–272 (May, 1904).

"Judge Tuly." *Charities,* 15:752–753 (March, 1906).

"Modern Lear—Strike at Pullman." *Survey,* 29:131–137 (November, 1912).

"My Experience as a Progressive Delegate." *McClures,* 40:12–14 (November, 1912).

"National Protection for Children." *Annals of the American Academy of Political and Social Sciences,* 29:57–60 (January, 1907).

"Newer Ideals of Peace." *Charities,* 17:599–606 (January, 1907).

"Operation of the Illinois Child Labor Law." *Annals of the American Academy of Political and Social Sciences,* 27:327–330 (March, 1906).

"Pragmatism in Politics." *Survey,* 29:11–12 (October, 1912).

"Present Crisis in Trades-Union Morals." *North American Review,* 179:178–193 (August, 1904).

"Probation Work Under Civil Service." *Charities,* 15:881–882 (March, 1906).

"Problems of Municipal Administration." *American Journal of Sociology,* 10:425–444 (January, 1905).

"Public Recreation and Social Morality." *Charities,* 18:492–494 (August, 1907).

"Recent Immigration." *Educational Review,* 29:245–263 (March, 1906).

"Religious Education and Contemporary Life." *Religious Education,* 6:145–152 (June, 1911).

"Respect for Law." *Independent,* 53:18–20 (January, 1901).

"Subtle Problems of Charity." *Atlantic,* 83:163–178 (February, 1899).

"Ten Years Experience in Illinois." *Annals of the American Academy of Political and Social Sciences,* 38:144–148 (Supplement, July, 1911).

"The Call of the Social Field." *Proceedings of the National Conference of Charities and Correction,* 1911, 370–372.

"The Challenge to the Contemporary Church." *Survey,* 28:195–198 (May 4, 1912).

"The Child at the Point of Greatest Pressure." *Proceedings of the National Conference of Charities and Correction,* 1912, 26–30.

"The College Woman and the Family Claim." *The Commons,* 29:3–9 (September, 1898).

"The Humanitarian Value of Civil Service." *Survey,* 28:14–16 (April, 1912).

"The New Party." *American Mercury,* 75:12–14 (November, 1912).

"The Reaction of Modern Life Upon Religious Education." *Religious Education,* 4:23–29 (April, 1909).

"The Reaction of Moral Instruction on Social Reform." *Survey,* 22:17–19 (August, 1909).

"The Significance of Organized Labor." *Women's World,* 1:551–557 (September, 1898).

"Trades Unions and Public Duty." *American Journal of Sociology,* 4:448–462 (January, 1898).

"Why Girls Go Wrong." *Ladies Home Journal,* 24:13–14 (September, 1907).

"Why the Ward Boss Rules." *Outlook,* 58:879–882 (April, 1898).

"Women's Work for Chicago." *Municipal Affairs,* 2:502–508 (September, 1898).

b. Articles by Albert J. Beveridge.

"Canada's Governmental Railway." *Review of Reviews,* 46:585–593 (November, 1912).

"Canada's System of Responsible Government." *McClures Magazine,* 37:330–337 (July, 1911).

"Canada's Tariff Policy—The Old East Versus the New West." *Review of Reviews,* 43:695–700 (June, 1911).

"Canadian Reciprocity, Its Influence on the Cost of Living." *Saturday Evening Post,* 183:3–5, 53–54 (March 25, 1911).

"Child Labor and the Nation." *Annals of the American Academy of Political and Social Sciences,* 29:115–124 (January, 1907).

"Development of a Colonial Policy." *Annals of the American Academy of Political and Social Sciences,* 30:3–15 (July, 1907).

"Federalism in Canada and the United States." *Review of Reviews,* 44:471–476 (October, 1911).

"Following Roosevelt as President." *Saturday Evening Post,* 177:1–3, 23 (September, 1904).

"Mutual Confidence and Consideration." *Reader,* 10:377–386 (September, 1907).

"Nation." *Reader,* 9:356–436 (March, 1907).

"National Integrity." *Reader,* 7:569–573 (May, 1906).

"Our Canadian Cousins. How They Break Their Trusts to Harness." *Saturday Evening Post,* 184:10–11, 44–45 (July, 1911).

"Our Canadian Cousins. How They Handle Their Currency Problems." *Saturday Evening Post,* 183:3–5, 40–42 (June 17, 1911).

"Our Canadian Cousins. How They Handle Their Immigration Problems." *Saturday Evening Post,* 184:9–10 (August, 1911).

"Our Canadian Cousins. How They Solve the Problems of Industrial Wars." *Saturday Evening Post,* 184:26–27, 74 (September, 1911).

"Our Canadian Cousins. Profiting by Our Mistakes." *Saturday Evening Post,* 184:26–28, 53 (September, 1911).

"Our Canadian Cousins. The History of a Railroad Triumvirate." *Saturday Evening Post,* 184:10–12, 32–33 (July, 1911).

"Permanent Tariff Commission." *Annals of the American Academy of Political and Social Sciences,* 32:409–428 (September, 1908).

"Regulation not Extermination." *Reader,* 9:579–588 (May, 1907).

"The Fifth Wheel in Our Government." *Century,* 79:208–214 (December, 1909).

"The Government of Dependencies." *Reader,* 10:259–269 (August, 1907).

"The Insurgents." *Saturday Evening Post*, 182:3–5, 58–60 (October 16, 1909).

"The Nation Versus States' Rights." *Reader*, 9:465–471 (April, 1907).

"The Position of Child Labor Legislation." *Independent*, 62:434–436 (February, 1907).

"True Liberty Under Law." *Reader*, 10:148–156 (July, 1907).

"Trusts and Their Treatment." *Reader*, 10:40–46 (June, 1907).

c. *Articles by William Jennings Bryan.*

"Trusts and Their Treatment." *Reader*, 10:34–40 (June, 1907).

"Prevention More Than Penalty." *Reader*, 11:145–151 (January, 1908).

d. *Articles published by the Civic Federation of Chicago.*

Analysis of Chicago Market Milk. [Chicago?], 1904.

A Summary of the Reports of the Special State Tax Commission. [Chicago?], 1907.

Bi-ennial Report, 1905. Chicago, 1905.

Bi-ennial Report, 1907. Chicago, 1907.

Bi-ennial Report, October, 1911. [Chicago?], 1911.

Bi-ennial Report of the Executive Committee. Chicago, 1909.

Chicago and the Constitution. [Chicago?], 1902.

Chicago Conference on Trusts. Chicago, 1900.

Chicago Gas Trust Bills, Another Attack on the People. Desperate Efforts to Legalize and Perpetuate a Practical Monopoly. [Chicago?], 1907.

Dangers of the Initiative and Referendum. [Chicago?, 1911?]

First Annual Report of the Central Council, 1894-1895. [Chicago?, 1895?].

Legislative Report, 1911. [Chicago?], 1911.

Saving Lives with Pictures. [Chicago?, 1910?].

Tax Facts for Illinois. [Chicago?], 1912.

Tax Inequities in Illinois. Chicago, 1910.

The Civic Federation of Chicago, What It Has Accomplished. [Chicago?, 1899?].

The Initiative and Referendum. A Public Danger. [Chicago?, 1911?].

The New Chicago Charter, Why it Should be Adopted at the Special Election September 17. [Chicago?], 1907.

The Street Railways of Chicago. [Chicago?], 1901.

e. *Articles by Samuel Gompers.*

"Chinese Exclusion." *Independent*, 56:947–948 (April, 1904).

"Editorials." *American Federationist*, 1–19 (1894–1912).

"Free Speech and the Injunction Order." *Annals of the American Academy of Political and Social Sciences*, 36:255–264 (September, 1910).

"Judicial Invasion of Guaranteed Rights." *American Federationist*, 17:298–300 (April, 1910).

"Labor's Struggle for the Right to Organize." *Outlook*, 97:267–270 (February, 1911).

"Lessons of the Recent Strike." *North American Review*, 159:201–206 (August, 1894).

"Ministers Debate Labor." *American Federationist,* 9:438–440 (August, 1902).

"Organized Labor's Attitude Toward Child Labor." *Annals of the American Academy of Political and Social Sciences,* 27:337–341 (May, 1906).

"President Gompers in Europe." *American Federationist,* 17:144–148, 243–245 (February, March, 1910).

"Stroles and the Coal Miners." *Forum,* 24:27–33 (September, 1897).

"The Attitude of Labor Toward Governmental Regulation of Industry." *Annals of the American Academy of Political and Social Sciences,* 32:75–81 (July, 1908).

"The Limitations of Conciliation and Arbitration." *Annals of the American Academy of Political and Social Sciences,* 20:27–34 (July, 1902).

La Follette, Robert M. "Editorials." *La Follette's Magazine,* 1–4 (1909–1912).

f. Articles by Edgar Gardner Murphy.

Alabama's First Question. Montgomery, 1902.

"Backward or Forward?" *South Atlantic Quarterly,* 8:19–38 (January, 1909).

Federal Regulation of Child Labor. n.p., 1907.

"Freedman's Progress in the South." *Outlook,* 68:721–724 (July, 1901).

Race Problems of the South. n.p., [1905?].

"Reconstruction in Religion." *Outlook,* 67:682–686 (March, 1901).

"Shall the Fourteenth Amendment Be Enforced?" *North American Review,* 180:109–133 (January, 1905).

Short Letter on the Southern Question. n.p., 1907.

Southern Education in its National Aspects. n.p., 1902.

"Southern Prosperity is not Shackled to Child Labor." *Charities,* 10:453–456 (May, 1903).

"Task of the Leader." *Sewanee Review,* 15:1–30 (January, 1907).

The Church and the Negro Episcopate. n.p., 1907.

"The National Child Labor Committee." *Charities,* 12:574–576 (June, 1904).

The Peonage Cases in Alabama. n.p., 1901.

The South and Her Children. n.p., 1903.

The White Man and the Negro at the South. n.p., 1900.

"With the Jails." *Charities,* 18:290 (June, 1907).

PRIMARY SOURCES: OFFICIAL PUBLICATIONS

State of Wisconsin. *Senate Journals.* Madison, 1901, 1903, 1905.
.... *Assembly Journals.* Madison, 1901, 1903, 1905.
Congressional Record. Washington, 1899–1912.
Proceedings of the Annual Convention of the American Federation of Labor. Various places, 1890–1912.

SECONDARY SOURCES: BOOKS

Aaron, Daniel. *Men of Good Hope: A Study of American Progressives.* New York, 1951.

Bean, Walton. *Boss Reuf's San Francisco.* Berkeley, 1952.

Beard, Charles and Mary. *The Rise of American Civilization.* 2 volumes. New York, 1937.

Blum, John M. *The Republican Roosevelt.* Cambridge, 1954.

Bowers, Claude G. *Beveridge and the Progressive Era.* New York, 1932.

Bremner, Robert H. *From the Depths.* New York, 1956.

Cremin, Lawrence A. *The Transformation of the School.* New York, 1962.

Croly, Herbert. *The Promise of American Life.* New York, 1909.

Curti, Merle. *The Making of an American Community: A Case Study of Democracy in a Frontier County.* Stanford, 1959.

Curti, Merle and Vernon Carstenson. *The University of Wisconsin: A History, 1848–1925.* 2 volumes. Madison, 1949.

Destler, Charles McA. *American Radicalism, 1865–1901.* Menasha, Wisconsin, 1946.

DeVoto, Bernard. *The Literary Fallacy.* Boston, 1944.

Dulles, Foster R. *Labor in America.* New York, 1949.

Farlie, John A. *A Report on the Taxation and Revenue System in Illinois, prepared for the Special Tax Commission of the State of Illinois.* Danville, 1910.

Fine, Sidney. *Laissez-faire and the General Welfare State, 1865–1901.* Ann Arbor, 1956.

Flinn, Joseph. *Handbook of Chicago Biography.* Chicago, 1893.

Forcey, Charles. *The Crossroads of Liberalism.* New York, 1961.

Fox, Dixon Ryan, editor. *Sources of Culture in the Middle West.* New York, 1934.

Fromm, Erich. *The Sane Society.* New York, 1955.

Grant, Bruce. *Fight for a City.* Chicago, 1955.

Haig, Robert M. *A History of the General Property Tax in Illinois.* Urbana, 1914.

Hofstadter, Richard. *The Age of Reform.* New York, 1955.

.... *Social Darwinism in America, 1860–1915.* Philadelphia, 1944.

Hutchinson, William T., editor. *Marcus W. Jernegan Essays in American Historiography.* Chicago, 1937.

Illinois, University of. *Illinois State Revenue, 1895–1920.* Urbana, 1922.

Jones, Ernest. *Sigmund Freud.* 3 volumes. London, 1953–1957.

Karson, Marc. *American Labor Movement and Politics, 1900–1918.* Carbondale, Illinois, 1958.

Kent, Elizabeth. *William Kent, Independent.* n.p., [1950?].

King, Hoyt. *Citizen Cole of Chicago.* Chicago, 1931.

La Follette, Belle C. and Fola. *Robert M. La Follette.* 2 volumes. New York, 1953.

Leonard, John W. *A Book of Chicagoans.* Chicago, 1905.

Lewis, Lloyd and Henry Justin Smith. *Chicago, The History of Its Reputation.* New York, 1929.

Link, Arthur. *Woodrow Wilson and the Progressive Era.* New York, 1954.

Linn, James Weber. *Jane Addams.* New York, 1935.

McCarthy, Charles. *The Wisconsin Idea.* New York, 1912.

Mann, Arthur. *Yankee Reformers in an Urban Age.* Cambridge, 1954.

Maxwell, Robert S. *La Follette and the Rise of the Progressives in Wisconsin.* Madison, 1956.

May, Henry F. *Protestant Churches and Industrial America.* New York, 1949.

.... *The End of American Innocence.* New York, 1959.

Miller, William D. *The Progressive Movement in Memphis.* Memphis, 1957.

Mowry, George E. *The California Progressives.* Berkeley, 1951.

.... *Theodore Roosevelt and the Progressive Movement.* Madison, 1946.

.... *The Era of Theodore Roosevelt.* New York, 1958.

Murphy, Maude K. *Edgar Gardner Murphy.* New York, 1943.

Noble, Ransom W. *New Jersey Progressivism Before Wilson.* Princeton, 1946.

Pollack, Norman. *The Populist Response to Industrial America.* Cambridge, 1962.

Rayback, Joseph G. *A History of American Labor.* New York, 1959.

Reed, Louis S. *The Labor Philosophy of Samuel Gompers.* New York, 1930.

Sutherland, Douglas. *Fifty Years on the Civic Front.* Chicago, 1943.

Syrett, Harold C. *The City of Brooklyn, 1865-1898.* New York, 1945.

Taft, Phillip A. *The A.F. of L. in the Time of Gompers.* New York, 1957.

Turner, Frederick Jackson. *The Frontier in American History.* New York, 1920.

Wendt, Lloyd and Herman Kogan. *Lords of the Levee: The Story of Bath House John and Hinky Dink.* Indianapolis, 1943.

White, Morton G. *Social Thought in America.* New York, 1949.

Wiebe, Robert H. *Businessmen and Reform: A Study of the Progressive Movement.* Cambridge, 1962.

Woodward, C. Vann. *Origins of the New South.* Baton Rouge, 1951.

Zink, Howard. *City Bosses in the United States.* Durham, 1930.

SECONDARY SOURCES: ARTICLES

Abbott, Edith. "Grace Abbott and Hull House." *Social Service Review,* 24:374-394, 493-518 (September, December, 1950).

.... "Hull House of Jane Addams." *Social Service Review,* 26:334-338 (September, 1952).

Baker, Ray S. "The Civic Federation of Chicago." *Outlook,* 52:132–133 (July, 1895).

Braeman, John. "The Rise of Albert J. Beveridge to the United States Senate." *Indiana Magazine of History,* 53:355–382 (December, 1957).

Chandler, Alfred D., Jr. "The Origins of Progressive Leadership," in Elting E. Morrison, editor, *The Letters of Theodore Roosevelt,* 8:1462–1465 (Cambridge, 1954).

Coffin, John A. "The Senatorial Career of Albert J. Beveridge." *Indiana Magazine of History,* 24:139–185, 242–294 (September, December, 1928).

Commons, John R. "Karl Marx and Samuel Gompers." *Political Science Quarterly,* 41:281–286 (June, 1926).

Curti, Merle. "Jane Addams on Human Nature." *Journal of the History of Ideas,* 22:240–253 (April–June, 1961).

Doherty, Herbert J. "Voices of Protest from the New South." *Mississippi Valley Historical Review,* 42:45–66 (June, 1955).

Going, Allen J. "The Reverend Edgar Gardner Murphy. His Ideas and Influence." *The Historical Magazine of the Protestant Episcopal Church,* 25:391–402 (December, 1956).

Greene, John C. "Objectives and Methods in Intellectual History." *Mississippi Valley Historical Review,* 44:58–74 (June, 1957).

Hacker, Louis. "Sections—or Classes." *Nation,* 137:108–110 (July, 1926).

Link, Arthur S. "The Progressive Movement in the South." *North Carolina Historical Review,* 23:172–195 (April, 1946).

Mandel, Bernard. "Samuel Gompers and the Negro Workers." *Journal of Negro History,* 40:34–60 (January, 1955).

Mann, Arthur. "Gompers and the Irony of Racism." *Antioch Review,* 12:203–214 (June, 1953).

Remy, Charles F. "The Election of Beveridge to the Senate." *Indiana Magazine of History,* 36:123–135 (June, 1940).

Riesman, David. "Their Tribe and Ours." *The New Republic,* 142:15–16 (February, 1960).

Scott, Andrew M. "The Progressive Era in Perspective." *Journal of Politics,* 21:685–701 (November, 1959).

Small, Albion W. "The Civic Federation of Chicago." *American Journal of Sociology,* 1:79–103 (July, 1895).

Titus, Warren I., editor. "The Senator and the Author, Beveridge-Churchill Correspondence." *Indiana Magazine of History,* 55:169–178 (June, 1959).

SECONDARY SOURCES: UNPUBLISHED DOCTORAL DISSERTATIONS

Disbrow, Donald W. The Progressive Movement in Philadelphia. University of Rochester, 1957.

Grob, Gerald N. Trade versus Reform Unionism: The Emergence of the

Modern American Labor Movement, 1865–1896. Northwestern University, 1958.

Roberts, Sidney J. Businessmen and Reform in Chicago, 1876–1900. Northwestern University. 1960.

Tree, Robert L. Victor Fremont Lawson and his Newspapers, 1890–1900. A Study of the Chicago *Daily News* and Chicago *Record*. Northwestern University, 1959.

Whipple, James B. Cleveland in Conflict, A Study in Urban Adolescence, 1876–1900. Western Reserve, 1951.

Index